Andrw Be

CW00455572

MAKING LOVE LAST

MAKING LOVE LAST

*How to Find and Keep
the Right Partner for You*

Bill & Lynne Hybels

Marshall Pickering
An Imprint of HarperCollinsPublishers

Marshall Pickering is an imprint of
HarperCollins*Religious*
Part of HarperCollins*Publishers*
77–85 Fulham Palace Road, London W6 8JB

Originally published under the title
Fit to be Tied by Zondervan Publishing House,
1415 Lake Drive, S.E., Grand Rapids,
Michigan 49506, USA

First published in Great Britain
in 1995 by Marshall Pickering

I   3   5   7   9   10   8   6   4   2

A catalogue record for this book
is available from the British Library

ISBN 0 551 02918 8

Printed and bound in Great Britain by
HarperCollinsManufacturing Glasgow

All scripture quotations, unless otherwise noted, are taken
from the *Holy Bible: New International Version* (North
American Edition). Copyright © 1973, 1978, 1984, by the
International Bible Society. Used by permission of
Zondervan Bible Publishers.

To Mr. and Mrs. K. K. Gregory,
for their remarkable friendship.
And to the staff and congregation of
Willow Creek Community Church,
for allowing us to minister
in the midst of our humanness.

Contents

Acknowledgments

When we signed the contract to write this book, we thought we were allowing ourselves ample time to complete the manuscript. Then came real life. One thing after the next interfered with our writing, and we became hopelessly behind schedule. We owe many thanks to Zondervan's Jim Buick, Scott Bolinder, and John Sloan. Jim and Scott watched more than one deadline pass unmet, and responded with grace. John again proved to be an insightful and patient editor; knowing how critical the editor/author relationship is, we thank God for him. During all our dealings with Zondervan, we felt like we were among friends.

Frequently during the writing process, we found it necessary to run away to a quiet place where we could think, talk, and work uninterrupted. Bob and Linda Buford, Rich and Helen DeVos, Jack and Clara Mains, and Ed and Elsa Prince generously provided beautiful places for us to run to. Grandma and Grandpa Barry and Greg and Corinne Ferguson lovingly covered the home front while we were away. Buster helped, too.

Jim Dethmer, Greg and Corinne Ferguson, and Russ Robinson helped tremendously by reading the manuscript and offering both encouragement and constructive criticism. This book is better for their careful attention to detail.

Though we'd love to, we can't take credit for the clever title of this book. Credit and our thanks go to Barbara McLennan who suggested "Fit to Be Tied" as the title for the sermon series out of which this book grew.

In recent months we've written many things about our marriage. Let us add just one more: Our marriage has produced two great kids. Each night when we tucked Todd into bed he prayed that "Mom and Dad would do a good job on the book." And Shauna's probing questions about what it was "really like" when we were dating brought to mind many memories that found their way onto the following pages.

MAKING LOVE LAST

Roller Coaster Romance

"*You're driving too fast* for road conditions."

"I've got it under control."

Our voices cut sharply above the speeding click of the windshield wipers.

For hours the sleet had pounded the windshield. For hours we had sat in bitter silence.

Thank God for the darkness. Thank God the kids slept quietly in the back of our blue and gray Suburban. Thank God we were almost home.

It should have been a wonderful Christmas vacation. Our Washington D.C. accommodations, reserved and paid for by a generous friend, were comfortable and roomy. The kids, feeling very grown-up at eleven (Shauna) and eight (Todd), enjoyed the freedom to roam alone through the huge old hotel which was nearly deserted because of the holidays; they were delighted to let Mom and Dad sleep in while they went downstairs to order breakfast on their own. Our tourist schedule was relaxed and modified to meet the kids' desires: their ideal afternoon balanced two hours at the Smithsonian with two hours in the hotel pool. Historic Georgetown was within walking distance, and each evening we strolled by the windows of quaint shops and chose from an assortment of curious eateries. One evening, while the boys "cruised" the town, the girls laughed and cried through Dickens' *A Christmas Carol* at the Ford Theater. Sounds wonderful, doesn't it?

For the kids it was—we hope; we did our best to create a memorable experience for them. But for us it was a dreadful week. Pleasant accommodations and a carefully planned itinerary could not ease the pain of our troubled marriage. The inviting king-sized bed in our private room could not bridge the gap between estrangement and intimacy. Frustration, loneliness, hopelessness, fear, despair, grief—they overshadowed every potential joy and defied every attempt to break through them. While the kids roamed we talked, but every conversation drove us further apart. We became increasingly dissatisfied with ourselves and angry at one another. We felt trapped, as we had so often in the past. Our commitments to the children, to the church, and to God kept us clinging to a marriage that all too often broke our hearts.

We drove into our driveway on the first day of the new year.

Happy New Year.

"I've never seen so many stars."

"It's like a black velvet dome studded with diamonds."

Lazy waves eased slowly up the sandy beach, then rolled back into the dark ocean waters. We lay on our backs on the sand, dreamy from the hypnotic rhythm of the gentle seas. There was not a hint of chill in the night air. Ah, to be cradled in creation.

The only thing that matched the perfection of that night was the day that had preceded it. We had awakened to a drizzly dawn, sipped lemon tea in our tiny rented cottage, then walked the beach toward the rainbow that arched in the south. The colors brightened while we watched, then faded as the morning sun sucked the moisture from the air. We walked waist deep in the water, then dove beneath the shimmering surface. We swam till our muscles ached, then let the buoyant swells carry us back toward shore. Tiny, silver slips of fish skimmed the surface of the water beside us, then flashed and dove and chased in an underwater playground of conches and clams and moon shells. Refreshed by our swim, we showered the salt from our hair, then dressed for the day in appropriate vacation attire—another swimsuit. We ate a late breakfast of granola and fruit, then each grabbed a book, scrunched sand and beach towels into chairlike mounds, and aimed our sunscreened faces toward the south.

The weather, with its cloudless sky, was at its best; and more importantly, we were at our best. The days of unrushed living had softened our rough edges and mellowed our intensities. We spoke softly and laughed easily. We traded books back and forth, insisting that the other read the "wonderful passages" we had just read. We compared notes and insights.

We reminisced and talked of the future. We revealed fears and acknowledged foibles and discussed dreams and shared secrets.

And the pleasure of that day gave way to romance beneath the stars.

Despair in the front seat of a Chevy Suburban? Or romance under a diamond sky? Which describes the real Hybels' marriage?

They both do. In fact, those two real-life episodes occurred within months of one another. It hardly seems possible, yet bouncing between those dramatic contrasts has been the pattern of our relationship since we met at seventeen. Our highs have been heartthrobbingly wonderful; our lows have been devastating. During the highs we think that meeting one another was the best thing that ever happened to us; during the lows we rue the day our paths crossed.

Let us tell you how it all began. . . .

Spring, 1969. J & D Roller Rink, Portage, Michigan. Ladies' Choice.

She watches him as she had done at several other Youth for Christ activities. He is blond and blue-eyed and handsome, with an air of confidence that intrigues her. She wonders if he has noticed her.

He has. And he is curious about the person behind the title of Michigan's Junior Miss. While she ponders whether or not to ask him to skate, he steals a quick glance at her, hoping she will ask.

She does, and it is not the only skate they share that evening. When the party ends they go their separate ways, but they have, without a doubt, "connected."

"Hey, Mom, I met this guy, Bill Hybels. I really like him. I hope I see him again."

Bill offers no similar comment to his mother, but he fully intends to see Lynne Barry again—soon.

Just days later, in a church parking lot in Kalamazoo, a group of high schoolers gathers to carpool to a YFC retreat at Spring Arbor College. Car assignments are made, and by some mysterious gift of fate, *she* ends up in the front seat of *his* car.

A country music fan, he tunes his radio to *Alabama's* nasal twang. A classical flutist, she chides him for his down-home taste. They laugh at their little difference, and talk nonstop for the next two hours, oblivious to their backseat riders.

The weekend schedule sends them both into musical competition—she in a flute trio, he in a small band where he sings and plays guitar and string bass. There is plenty of free time, however, and they use it well—quiet conversations in the deserted student lounge, long walks on country roads, an "against the rules" drive to a nearby town. They seem to have so much in common: They both love water sports—swimming, skiing, and especially sailing. And their fathers both fly airplanes and drive motorcycles. She hangs on every word while he tells of sailing across Lake Michigan in a furious rainstorm. He laughs at her comic adventure of learning to drive a motorbike—and crashing into a garbage can.

They talk, too, of more significant things: their shared faith, their commitment to ministry, their college plans, their values, their appreciation of their respective families. There seems to be so much potential in this relationship—and not *just* because they have a lot in common. There is something else, too.

It manifests itself in the laughter that punctuates every conversation, in the fun that surrounds every encounter, in the warmth that envelopes the entire weekend. There is a spark between them. There is magic. There is chemistry.

Too soon the weekend ends. But the next evening he calls her. She is teaching a private flute lesson, so she asks him to call again. By the time he calls back, she is being visited by another young man she has been dating, so she asks him to try again later. Angry at being put off, he decides to call one more time. If she refuses to take *this* call . . .

She doesn't. They plan their first official date.

It is Friday evening and they drive west on M-43 toward South Haven, a little resort town on the eastern shore of Lake Michigan. On the way they stop at an auction, for no particular reason except perhaps to hear the country music blasting from crude loudspeakers attached to the front of the dilapidated warehouse. Back in the car, they continue to the lake, park at South Beach, and walk barefoot across the sand and onto the pier. They sit beneath the red lighthouse that flashes its warning and watch the parade of boats that glide between the two concrete breakwaters to moor for the night. In the distant west, sails make sharp silhouettes against the pink and purple sunset.

While they sit and talk, a cool breeze drifts in. They scoot closer together to fend off the chill, grateful for an excuse to break through the reserve that separates them. Because of the fun of the previous weekend, this evening does not hold the normal discomforts of a first date. Still, there are the inevitable questions. *Is* she *having a good time? Is* he *having a good time? Should I hold her hand? Why doesn't he hold my hand?*

The truth is, they are both having a good time, and though she is somewhat disappointed when he does not request a good-night kiss, they both know they will be seeing much more of one another.

They date steadily throughout the summer. Twice a week, at least, he arrives at her house in the pickup truck he drives when he works on the farms owned by his father's produce company. It is a demanding summer job—long hours in hot, dusty, backbreaking conditions. But he has worked hard for his dad since he was five, and he takes it in stride. She is impressed with his sense of responsibility and his devotion to hard work and discipline. He is capable and motivated and goal oriented, and she respects that.

For him the dates are no small thing. It is not uncommon for him to work from sunup to past sundown; on the days they plan to meet he has to work extra hard to be able to leave before dark. It is an hour's drive from the farm to her house, and even before he starts the drive he is exhausted. Often he arrives at her house sweaty and caked with dust, straight from the fields, and she rides with him to his parents' home where he showers and dresses for the evening. Picking her up before he goes home saves a little time, and every extra moment counts. There is something about this girl that makes him want to grasp every possible moment to be with her. He appreciates her intelligence and depth, her gentleness and sensitivity.

What draws them together perhaps more than anything else is that they see one another as true peers. Neither feels "in charge" of their relationship. There is a mutuality of respect and appreciation that places them on an equal footing, and sets this relationship apart from any that either of them had known in the past.

By the end of summer they know this is a serious relationship. Unfortunately, in September she leaves for Wheaton College near Chicago; he stays in Kalamazoo to finish his last year of high school. The relationship turns into a series of anxious trips to the mailbox, late-night phone calls, and weekend visits, a pattern which continues for the next five years. Well, it doesn't exactly continue. In reality, it starts and stops—and starts again—repeatedly throughout those years. They are voluntary victims of a quintessential on-and-off-again romance, complete with a broken engagement and a year and a half of total separation.

I don't have to put up with this grief, she thinks, as she throws out his letters and shoves his graduation picture into a padded mailer.

I can be happier with someone else, he mumbles, as he fingers through the directory of women students at Dordt College in Sioux Center, Iowa.

But she cannot forget the wonderful moments that *hadn't* been touched by grief. And he finds out that he *isn't* happier with someone else.

So they try again, and find that they have grown during eighteen months apart. As individuals they are more mature, and that maturity translates into a more stable and satisfying relationship. They are married on May 18, 1974.

It is a grand occasion with all the usual trappings—and then some. By now, the twenty-two-year-old groom is the pastor of a growing youth ministry, and the "kids" seem to have taken over the wedding. With their youthful exuberance they have lent a kind of carnival atmosphere to a typically formal affair. Impatiently the bride and groom greet guests at the reception, anxious to leave the carnival behind and head for a Florida honeymoon.

They should have lingered at the carnival wedding; the honeymoon has a far less festive tone. They blame their irritability, their frequent arguments, and their emotional distance on their painfully sunburned bodies, but the real problem is their inability to resolve conflict.

A few months later they take a camping trip in upper

Michigan and have a marvelous time. They huddle together under waterfalls in the Tahquamenon River. They charge through the north woods on motorbikes. They hike along the sandy shores of Lake Superior. They call it their "real honeymoon" and forget their debacle in Florida. They see sunny days ahead.

But the storm clouds are rolling in again. The young husband's work proves to be a whirlwind that swirls faster and faster and sweeps away whatever gets in the way—like carefree walks on country roads, like leisurely breakfast conversations, like Friday night dates . . . like marriage.

So there are hurts and hostilities. There are sullen silences and angry outbursts. There are tears and fears and ultimatums.

And then, finally, there is brokenness. There are apologies and declarations of better intentions. There is hope. There is romance. There is, once again, a blissful string of highs.

To be followed by a new series of lows. It is not just the career demands that drive them into downward spirals. Over the years their differences have become pronounced and irritating. Oh, they still share their common values: They still bow before the same God and aim for the same life goals. But how differently they see the world. How differently they relate to other people. How differently they view marriage and family life. How differently they approach conflict. How differently they express love.

And how they misunderstand and judge one another. He feels like she is trying to reshape him to make him more acceptable to her. She feels like she has to be something she isn't in order to win his approval. They both despair of ever feeling consistently loved and accepted.

And so the story goes. From high to low to high to low again. Peaks and valleys connected by plateaus of longing and fear: longing for the next high, fear of the next low.

Writing of our marriage from a third-person perspective is more than a literary device. It is an attempt to gain insight into our marriage by standing outside it and looking at it objectively. For years we were mystified by the volatile nature of our relationship. Why were we so drawn to one another during that dusty summer of 1969? And why, with so many difficulties in our relationship, did we always decide to try again, even before the commitment of marriage held us together? On the other hand, why does our relationship spiral downward so easily? Why do we get so frustrated and so frequently reach painful impasses? If we love each other so much, why have we hurt each other so often?

Many hours of thinking, praying, and talking over these issues have taken some of the mystery out of those questions. We see now that we have been drawn together by some very strong compatibilities, but then almost simultaneously shoved apart by some very strong *in*compatibilities.

Fortunately, our areas of compatibility are of the absolutely essential kind—beliefs, goals, values, and character qualities related to the very essence of who we are as individuals—commonalities without which no relationship can thrive. The *plus* in our marriage is that, when all is said and done, we chose well. We each picked a life partner we could respect and relate to as an equal.

In the beginning these areas of compatibility were so obvious and heartwarming that we weren't even aware of the many incompatibilities that lurked beneath the surface. Fortunately, the incompatibilities were of a secondary nature—temperament differences and conflicting expectations—that could be negotiated and compromised and worked through. The problem was, we did not do that. We did not use our courtship as a time to ferret out our differences and come up with plans for dealing with them. We did not learn, until recent years, how to confront conflicts without wiping each other out in the process. The *minus* in our marriage was that we let a myriad of lesser incompatibilities nip away at our relationship day in and day out.

In addition, we each sabotaged the already challenging task of marriage-building by contributing our respective boatloads of personal sins and weaknesses—which ranged from workaholism to insecurity to distorted thinking to poor communication skills to misunderstandings of true spirituality. We eventually learned that an important piece in the marriage puzzle is to get our own lives in order, so we can be whole and healthy people. Anything that diminishes us as individuals diminishes the potential of our marriage. We both had to face a lot of internal ugliness and make radical changes in how we lived in order to become "fit" marriage partners. Years of fast pace and high pressure had made us both pretty awful people to live with.

Marriage is a humbling journey.

We have a twofold purpose in writing this book. First, we want to help single people choose their marriage partners wisely; we want to help them find partners with whom they share the absolutely crucial compatibilities. Second, we want to help married people stay married. We'll offer a two-pronged plan that includes: first, working through the lesser incompatibilities that interfere with peace and mutual satisfaction, and second, learning healthy patterns of living and relating on a daily basis.

At times it will be important for one or the other of us to tell a story or give our own particular viewpoint on some issue. So as not to confuse the reader, we have used the initials of our first names in the margin to indicate who is writing.

We are not experts on marriage. If anything qualifies us for writing this book, it is that we have suffered in our marriage. We have wished on more than one occasion that we could get out of our marriage. We have wondered how God let us make such a terrible mistake. We have felt hopeless and trapped.

And, in fact, we were trapped—by our own deeply held commitments. So we did the only thing that seemed right for us to do. We worked at it. And worked. And worked some more.

And we continue to work. Our union is still marked by high highs and low lows and probably will be for as long as we live. However, the highs are becoming more enjoyable and more frequent, and the lows are becoming less devastating and less frequent. And the thread of days and months upon which these contrasting moments hang is growing stronger all the time, reinforced again and again by memories and experiences that are increasingly pleasant and peace filled and satisfying.

Part One

On the Way to Marriage

One

Exposing the Marriage Myths

B As a teenager and young adult I prided myself in being disciplined. No matter how tired or sore I was after basketball practice I pushed myself to run another lap. No matter how late I stayed out on Friday night, I never failed to punch the produce company time clock at 6 A.M. on Saturday. No matter how much school I missed accompanying my dad on business trips, I always got my assignments done on time. No matter what was going on inside me, I usually exuded an air of confidence and strength. I was disciplined athletically, vocationally, academically, and—most importantly—emotionally. Nothing—and nobody—shook me; nothing "got to me." Neither my face nor my demeanor gave away the contents of my heart or mind. I could have been a professional poker player.

When it came to dating, I was careful never to let a girl know how much I cared. Consciously, I gave off signals that said, "I'm in control. You can't hurt me." Even with Lynne, whom I cared about very deeply, I kept my defenses up. In reality, what happened in our relationship—whether we were high or low—had an enormous effect on my life. To a great extent, the quality of my life depended on the quality of my relationship with Lynne. But I didn't let people—especially *her*—see that. I kept the seemingly impenetrable shield in place.

And it was a good thing. Because on a bitter cold December night in 1971 she did what no girl had done to me before. She blasted the foundation right out from under me.

Months earlier we had decided to get married. We had set the date, reserved the church, and begun attending to the myriad of details that go into planning a wedding. Then out of the blue, while we sat in my car in her parents'

B driveway, she dropped the bomb: "I don't have the peace of God regarding our marriage. I think we need to break up and part ways." She stepped out of my car—and out of my life.

True to my carefully controlled image, I closed the door, hit the road, and never looked back—at least on the outside. On the inside, I was crushed. Several days later I had to drive a produce truck to Detroit. On the way, Ray Price came on the radio singing "There Goes My Everything," and I watched the road through bleary eyes while I sang along . . . *there goes my reason for living . . . there goes my everything.*

My smooth exterior began showing more and more cracks, and my dad decided I needed a change of scenery. I had just quit college to join the family produce company, so my time was free. He sent me to South America for a month to visit several missionary families he knew. During sleepless nights on straw mats and sun-baked hours on sluggish riverboats, I had plenty of time to think. I thought first about the things I had said and done to drive Lynne away. I scrutinized our past conversations and tried to look at events through her eyes. I realized and lamented the foolishness of pretending to be tough. I determined that if Lynne would ever give me another chance, I would be more vulnerable, more sensitive, more tender toward her. If I never had that chance, at least I would apply the lessons I had learned to future relationships.

The time spent thinking brought perspective to my relational life. Time spent talking with godly missionaries brought a different, yet complementary perspective to my spiritual life. I began to see that I had allowed Lynne to become more central to my life than my relationship with Christ. I had not intended for that to happen, and I certainly had not let her see that. But slowly and subtly, my focus had shifted from the Lord to her.

God tells us in Exodus 20:5 that He is a "jealous God," not jealous in a petty, self-serving way, but jealous for our sakes. He knows that unless we give Him the place of preeminence He deserves, we will be frustrated, empty people. He knows that unless we honor Him as our

B ultimate need-meeter, we will entrust our needs to fallible
humans who will be unable to meet them.

After that broken engagement, I had to put my life back
together, which involved refocusing my confidence in my
relationship with Jesus Christ. I remember saying to
myself, "I can be happy single. Maybe God will lead me to
be single for the rest of my life. That's okay. He is
sufficient." That realization was key at that time in my life.
I became more serious about spiritual growth; I began to
develop and use my spiritual gifts; I got involved in lay
ministry. And I found life to be absolutely meaningful and
unbelievably joy filled.

A year and a half later, Lynne and I got back together. A
year after that we were married, with the clear and mutual
understanding that nothing would ever be more important
to either of us than our relationship with Jesus Christ.
Though focusing our attention on Him did not resolve all
our differences or solve all our relational problems, it did
give us a firm foundation upon which to build a marriage.

But what if the story hadn't ended this way? What if it
had been a story of lifelong singleness? I firmly believe God
would have continued to be sufficient, life would have
continued to be full, and I would have continued to know
the joy I felt as a twenty-one-year-old first acknowledging
the preeminence of God. God's promises of joy and peace
and satisfaction are not made just to married people. He
doesn't say, "I came to give abundant life to those of you
who are married." He offers that to anyone—married or
unmarried—who has a relationship with Him.

*God offers His promises of joy and peace and satisfaction to
anyone—married or unmarried—who has a relationship with Him.*
From a biblical standpoint, those words cannot be denied. But
how many single people really, deep down inside, believe them?
Do they rejoice in that truth? Or do they voice those words with
a ring of resignation?

Observation indicates that very few people actually consider singleness as an acceptable option, let alone an example of
abundant living.

In spite of the fact that over fifty percent of marriages end up as dashed dreams, Americans are still in love with marriage. Experts estimate that ninety-five percent of today's unmarried people still deeply desire to be married. Census figures reveal that only about five percent of people over sixty-five years old have remained "never married."[1] Almost everybody wants to marry, plans to, and eventually does.

Unfortunately, they often do so for the wrong reasons.

THE PRESSURE MOUNTS

Some yield to external pressure. It usually begins during the second or third year of college when girls burst into their friends' dorm rooms, ring fingers first—flashing their glittering symbols of eternal love. The friends, who are not as excited as they appear, begin to feel the subtle pressure. *Who is next? Why isn't it me? Last girl loses, and I don't want to be a loser.*

Parental pressure can be as strong as the peer pressure. Most parents don't mean it, but the comments made in fun during the teen years aren't so funny when the son or daughter approaches the mid-twenties. "When are you going to start looking for a wife?" "You must not be husband-shopping in the right places." Loose references to "unclaimed jewels" strike terror in the hearts of young women wanting desperately to be claimed; young men weary of their "freedom" cringe at jokes about independent bachelors.

The underlying belief that all unmarried people feel cheated or bitter drives well-meaning friends and family to suggest blind dates for young adults "unfortunate enough" to be unmarried at twenty-five. Their solicitous concern shouts an ugly question: *What's wrong with you?*

Unfortunately, many unmarried people begin to internalize the unspoken questions and doubt their worth or acceptability. *What is wrong with me?* they wonder. *Is it my personality? Is it my appearance? Is it my level of intelligence? Is it my degree of competence? Is it my lifestyle?* Commercial advertisers prey on—and heighten—the insecurities of single people. Televised ads portray a timid, rejected loser doubting the value of his existence. In desperation he buys the right deodorant—or tie, or shirt, or cologne, or hair spray, or car—and overnight he is transformed into a macho, confident, middleweight boxing contender, fighting off the girls. The point is clear. *Our product can fix your problem. Then you can have girlfriends and get married like normal people do.*

Society's underlying message—that there is something wrong with people who are not married or in serious dating relationships—pushes single people to fret and flirt and market themselves. Too often they hurl themselves at the first candidate who comes along.

Ellen Rothman suggests additional reasons why people want to get married: to have children, to get even with an old lover, to get out of the parental home, to further a career, to obtain a father or mother for their children. Others marry for money, power, security, prestige, or readily available sex. Still others marry simply so they can say they did.[2]

GOOD-BYE LONELY DAYS

Unfortunately, there are even more wrong reasons to marry. Some of these reasons are touted as inevitable benefits of marriage; in reality, they are nothing more than myths. The first myth that motivates some people to marry is this: Marriage will end my aloneness.

A single person wrote this about her struggle with loneliness: "I can't think of anything I hate more than being alone. Everywhere I turn I see couples—couples on television, couples in cars, couples on planes, couples in restaurants. Everywhere there are reminders that I am alone. I wonder if I will ever find a person to fill that hole in my heart."

I wonder if I will ever find a person to fill that hole in my heart. That line is a flashing warning signal. Apparently this woman, like many others, is dreaming of a knight on a white horse who will gallop into her life and rescue her from the gnawing ache in her soul. She is longing for a human being who will offer her perfect intimacy. She is crying out for someone who will understand her fully, accept her unconditionally, and end her sense of isolation. The right man, she believes, can forever end her aloneness—can fill the hole in her heart. Behind her words rumbles the myth that too many young men and women believe: that marriage is the cure-all for human loneliness.

The truth is, there are millions of desperately lonely

married people. They may share a table, a sofa, and even a bed
with their marriage partner, but they still feel lonely. They may
even have an ideal marriage—a genuinely intimate and loving
relationship—and still feel lonely deep inside.

Did they marry the wrong person? Build a shallow
marriage? Or did they simply place an unrealistic demand on
marriage? Perhaps they failed to understand that God created
human beings to yearn for two levels of relational intimacy. The
first level can be met by establishing a deep, honest, trusting
relationship with a friend or marriage partner. The *second level*
can only be met by entering into an authentic, growing
relationship with God.

Most unmarried people are conscious of their first level of
yearning—for a close relationship with another human being.
But their second level of yearning, their longing to be intimate
with God, is often buried beneath the surface of their conscious
awareness; they feel it, but don't understand it. So the two
yearnings get "mixed"; they get lumped together in one giant
gnawing need. The result is a doubled drive—an obsession,
sometimes—to find the person who can satisfy *all* the intimacy
needs. Clearly, that is a setup for heartbreak.

Some of these singles never find partners and live with
constant loneliness and frustration. Others do marry, but they
may be even worse off. Six months into marriage they discover
that some of their intimacy needs are still unmet. Then what?
They pressure their spouses to meet not only the level one needs
they feel consciously, but also the level two needs they feel
subconsciously. If they are not careful, they destroy the
relationship by putting too much pressure on it—by expecting
human beings to meet intimacy needs that only God can meet.

Fifty years ago divorce was considered a tragedy. Divorced
people would do anything to avoid discussion of their marital
status. Today, people readily admit they have been divorced—
not once, not twice, but three or four times. What does it
matter? Who is counting? It is called serial monogamy. It is men
and women moving from relationship to relationship looking
for a single individual to meet all their intimacy needs. It is men
and women failing to understand that a marriage partner can
meet, at best, only part of their intimacy needs.

How can marriages *not* fail when we expect them to do

something beyond the realm of possibility? A good marriage to the right person, entered into under God's direction and nurtured carefully, can go a long way toward meeting the human need for intimacy; the Bible calls that oneness. But within every human heart there remains a hole that only God can fill.

There are millions of people—married and unmarried—wandering around this globe with painful yearnings that could be met if they would spend less time seeking human companionship and more time seeking God. Jesus said in John 10:10, "I have come that they may have life, and have it to the full." A spouse may provide a little icing for the cake, but only God, through Jesus Christ, can provide the foundation for a full and meaningful life.

Jesus said in John 14:27, "Peace I leave with you; my peace I give you. I do not give to you as the world gives. Do not let your hearts be troubled and do not be afraid." No spouse or lover can say that. The honeymoon doesn't last for long; before you know it, real life comes crashing in with all its fury and challenge. Then who provides peace in the midst of the storm? Who takes away the fear?

In Matthew 11:28 Jesus says, "Come to me, all you who are weary and burdened, and I will give you rest." Do you know you have a restless soul? Do you realize how often that restlessness drives you? How often it pushes you into accomplishments, pursuits, even relationships? No friend, lover, or spouse can offer soul-satisfaction. Only Jesus Christ offers the internal rest, the calmness, the true fullness of life that can free us from the relentless drive toward superficial satisfaction.

Even that illusive yet longed for state we call *joy* is more a byproduct of a spiritual relationship than a human one. Galatians 5:22 tells us that joy is a fruit borne by the work of the Holy Spirit. It is tied not to external circumstances, such as singleness or marriage, but to internal circumstances—the presence of God's spirit within us.

So what is the point for single people? Plumb the depths of your relationship with Jesus Christ. Before you plunge into a human relationship with expectations that can never be met, build a solid foundation with Christ. Internalize His peace, His rest, His joy. Allow Him to meet the needs that even the most ideal man or woman on earth will never be able to meet. Then you can approach dating and marriage from a position of fullness rather than emptiness, from a state of satisfaction rather than desperation.

PUT ME BACK TOGETHER

One major advantage we had in approaching spouse selection was that our views of ourselves and of marriage were largely positive. While no human being has grown up in a perfect home, we each grew up in a relatively stable, loving, healthy environment. Neither of us had been scarred by alcoholism or divorce or neglect or abuse. Neither of us felt unloved or unaccepted. And all four of our parents were devoted followers of Christ who were committed to the church, to personal integrity, to biblical values, and to family life. True, we each had our fair share of weaknesses, misbeliefs, and immaturities that complicated our marriage; these will be acknowledged more openly in later chapters. But, in broad terms, we were basically healthy individuals with realistic expectations of marriage.

Unfortunately that is not true for many people today. Record numbers of young people are growing up in unloving, unhappy homes. More and more families are being shattered by divorce, devastated by alcoholism, and ravaged by emotional and physical abuse. Young people growing up in such situations often carry wounds that no one sees, wounds that leave them hurt and needy, wounds that drive them to search for someone who can heal them, patch up their broken places, or at least make their pain subside for a while.

Consciously, these wounded people look for spouses. Unconsciously, they look for healers. They believe a second myth: Marriage will heal my brokenness. In an age of unprecedented brokenness, this is a dangerous myth.

A young person who was neglected, devalued, or mistreated during his growing-up years often feels like he is drowning emotionally. Feelings swirl around inside of him so fast he fears he will get sucked under and never be able to come up. Just then a five-foot four-inch blond-haired life preserver floats by. The young man does what any drowning person would do: He grabs on for dear life. *Maybe she can help me. Maybe she can save me from drowning.* The five-foot four-inch blond interprets this young man's tight embrace as true love. True love! The storybook kind. The kind that will last a lifetime. The kind she has been searching for.

After a sermon in which this metaphor was used, a woman named Sheila said through her tears, "I almost vomited when I heard the part about someone reaching out for a life preserver. That's what happened to me, but I didn't understand it until I heard it described today. I've only been married a few months. I thought it was true love. Nobody ever reached out to me the way this man did. Nobody ever called me as often or dated me as passionately as this man did. Nobody ever wrote the kind of notes this man did. Nobody ever hugged and embraced and hung onto me the way this man did. I was *sure* it was true love. But just last Monday night my husband beat me up. He accused me of drifting away from him!"

A man or woman who latches onto a life preserver, dates ferociously for a few months, then gets married, is opening the door for disaster. One day the life-preserving spouse is going to get out of bed and say, "Please, can you give me just a little slack? Can you give me a little space? You've been clutching me so tightly I'm losing my breath." And that pain-filled, drowning spouse is going to interpret that request for space as another round of rejection, or neglect, or abuse—and the threat will be too much to bear. The marriage will go up for grabs.

B Though I do few weddings now, earlier in my ministry I did all the weddings at our church. Sometimes there were three or four weddings per weekend. I would stand with my Bible open, explaining God's guidelines for marriage. The radiant young woman and the excited young man would stand within fourteen inches of me, meeting my gaze with a beam of shared love and passion and electricity. Incredible! Then they would repeat their vows of lifelong devotion and float out of the chapel. Six months later they would crash like a plane out of the sky. Devastated. Crushed. Another dashed dream.

Why did that happen? Because they thought they could

heal one another's brokenness. Maybe they were both wounded, maybe just one was. But whole, healthy marriages cannot be built on foundations of brokenness. Spouses cannot be expected to be life preservers.

TOO MUCH LOVE

Recently a woman named Mary and a friend of hers approached us after a service at our church. Mary said, "I'm living with a man, and I know I shouldn't be. So I'm going to marry him . . . I think. There are a few problems, though. My friend keeps telling me I shouldn't go through with the wedding, but I want to know what you think."

She proceeded to tell us of her boyfriend's drinking problem, his cocaine use, his frequent unemployment, his temper, and finally, his verbal and physical abuse toward her. She looked at us expectantly.

It didn't take much thought to decide how to respond. "Listen well, Mary. Please listen. You are living immorally with an unemployed, cocaine-snorting alcoholic who abuses you emotionally and beats you physically. Don't even think about marrying him. In fact, don't even go back to your apartment. Have your friend pick up your clothes for you. Don't even go back there. And Mary, you need to get help. You need to see a counselor. You should never again let anyone treat you that way!"

Our hearts broke for a woman so wounded inside that she seriously considered marrying a man whose own life was destroyed and who wanted to destroy hers. Why did she do it? Experts agree that people like Mary usually come from dysfunctional families where their emotional needs were not met. They are so desperate to be loved and accepted, so lacking in self-esteem and fearful of being abandoned, that they will cling to *any* relationship, even one that brings them pain. Looking for a marriage that will heal their brokenness, they just become more and more broken.

NOT A VICTIMLESS CRIME

People who think marriage will heal their brokenness end up either becoming victims as Mary did, or victimizing their spouses as Sheila's husband did. But it does not have to be this way. If you are single, please use this two-pronged approach to avoid getting involved in a destructive marriage.

First, be ruthlessly honest about your own brokenness. Do you feel like you are drowning inside? Are you looking for a life preserver? Are you carrying hurts and disappointments that you secretly hope a spouse can heal? Do you have unfinished business with parents or others that you need to resolve before you can build a healthy relationship? Is your self-esteem so poor, because of past mistreatment, that you would be vulnerable to an abusive or destructive marriage?

If you answered yes to any of those questions, please put the issue of dating and marriage on the back burner. Face first things first. Deal with your brokenness. Make your own healing a priority. Get introspective, analyze the past, seek counsel. The only thing worse than being a single broken person is being a married broken person.

Second, if you want to avoid serious trouble, you must observe potential mates very carefully. Look below the surface. What kind of expectations do potential mates have? What excess baggage are they carrying? What unfinished business do they need to resolve with their parents? What is their agenda? Are they looking for a healthy, mutual relationship? Or for a life preserver? A miracle worker? A healer?

The key to answering these questions accurately is obvious. Time. If you have a problem with long courtships, you might as well close this book right now. You see, we have a real problem with people jumping into marriage prematurely. It is not just a matter of principle. It is simply that we have seen too much pain.

DOUBLE YOUR PLEASURE?

Probably the most widely believed of all the marriage myths is this one: Marriage will ensure my happiness. It is almost accepted as fact that a quick walk down the center aisle will usher one into the halls of happiness. The real truth is, it might, and it might not.

The mistaken assumption is that a wedding will automatically change a person. But that seldom happens. In most cases, an unhappy single person will be an unhappy married person. A bitter, angry single person will be a bitter, angry married person. A greedy single person will be a greedy married person. An impatient single person will be an impatient married person. Marriage does not produce life or character transformations. Such changes are produced by the inner work of the Holy Spirit, which is not dependent on one's marital status.

This myth seems ridiculous indeed when you consider the math of marriage: One sinner plus another sinner equals two sinners. Double trouble under one roof. Add a couple "sinner-lings," and we're talking quadruple trouble under that same single roof.

In the covenant of marriage God asks two self-willed sinners to come together and become one flesh—not in body only, but in spirit, in attitude, in communication, in love. Think about the implications. Imagine two self-willed sinners trying to submit to one another as God calls them to do. That will take a decade. Or imagine two self-willed sinners trying to serve one another joyfully. Another decade. Imagine two self-willed sinners trying to show honor to one another. Yet another decade. Or to encourage one another. Or to edify one another. It is a lifetime challenge—perhaps the single greatest challenge there is.

And, as we said in the previous chapter, there are so many little issues that can complicate the challenge. Even mature, well-adjusted, Spirit-filled believers have to work through countless areas of disparity. There is financial disparity: He wants golf clubs; she wants a dishwasher. There is recreational disparity: She wants to travel; he wants to plant a garden. There is sexual disparity: He is romantically inclined tonight; she was last night. There is social disparity: She favors her friends; he favors his. Every time you turn around there is a new area of potential disagreement.

Don't misunderstand us. Marriage can be wonderful. It can be deeply satisfying and mutually fulfilling. But, *if* it becomes that, it is because *both* partners have paid a very high price over many years to make it that way. They will have died to selfishness a thousand times. They will have had countless difficult conversations. They will have endured sleepless nights and strained days. They will have prayed hundreds of prayers for wisdom and patience and courage and understanding. They will have said "I'm sorry" too many times to remember. They will have been stretched to the breaking point often enough to have learned that, unless Christ is at the center of both their lives, the odds for achieving marital satisfaction are very, very low.

Marriage a ticket to happiness? Not on your life. If this book accomplishes nothing else, we hope it dispels the naive and destructive notion that marriage is easy and that it guarantees happiness. Most unmarried people have no idea what it takes to make a marriage work; they grossly underestimate the price people have to pay to build long-term, mutually satisfying relationships. And they fail to understand that the only people with the strength to pay that price are those who have plumbed the depths of their relationship with God, have dealt with their own brokenness, and have reached a place of happiness within the context of their singleness.

NOT FOR EVERYONE

The final myth about marriage is that it is God's plan for everyone. It isn't. The Bible acknowledges that some believers will choose not to marry. In Matthew 19:12 Jesus defends those who "have renounced marriage because of the kingdom of heaven." To these people God will give the capacity to remain single for a lifetime and to enjoy that state—the "gift of singleness" it might be called.

He does not say that those who choose singleness are more spiritual than those who choose marriage. But he does affirm and legitimize their decision. Scripture mentions a host of good reasons for remaining single, but we would like to look at just two.

First, people who marry will have additional trouble in life—double trouble, as we've already noted. Says the apostle Paul of the extra trouble caused by marriage: "I want to spare you this" (1 Cor. 7:28). Given the context in which Paul's letter was written, the comment makes perfect sense. The Christians at Corinth were notoriously immature, and nostril deep in struggles with idol worship, elevation of church leaders, division in the church, drunkenness at the communion table, lawsuits against one another, and confusion over spiritual gifts. "The last thing you people need," says Paul, "is marriage. Any more trouble, and you'll go right over the ledge. You better look before you leap." Many single people today are no less steeped in confusion, trouble, and immaturity than were the Corinthians. Perhaps for them, too, singleness is the best option—at least for a time.

The second reason for remaining single is the problem of divided devotion. Paul reminds the Corinthians that an unmarried man or woman is free to be concerned with how he or she can please the Lord, but a married person must be concerned with pleasing his or her spouse. "I am saying this for your own good," he says, "not to restrict you, but that you may live in a right way in undivided devotion to the Lord" (1 Cor. 7:35).

> **B** I can't count how many times I have been in the midst of fruitful message preparation, with books and papers strewn across my desk, when I have looked at the clock and realized that Lynne has dinner waiting and the kids are beginning to wonder where their dad is. In Scripture I am called to be a godly husband and father, so I close the books and go home. I do not have the freedom to be undistractedly devoted to the work of the kingdom that I had before I was married.

We are not talking here about more or less love for Christ. Married people can love Christ every bit as much as unmarried people can. The issue is a practical one of time and energy to invest in kingdom concerns. Most single people have more free hours to invest in service than most married people do.

That doesn't mean every single person should choose to remain single forever. It does mean, however, that every single person should submit his or her singleness to God, and use this era of freedom, for as long as it lasts, to serve God unhindered.

A REALITY CHECK

We have a high view of marriage. We believe our marriage was God ordained, and that over the years it has been God sustained. It has been both a tool that God has used to challenge and shape us and a gift that He has given to encourage and refresh us. Every year we sense the increasing value of our growing relationship.

But we also have a realistic view. We don't believe it is the answer for everyone. And while it has added a profoundly meaningful dimension to our lives, it did not satisfy our deepest human needs. It did not cure our inner loneliness. It did not heal our brokenness. It did not ensure our happiness.

It will not do that for you either. It does not promise to.

Notes

[1]Harold Ivan Smith, *Single and Feeling Good* (Nashville: Abingdon Press, 1987), 9.

[2]Ellen K. Rothman, *Hands and Hearts: A History of Courtship in America*; cited in Smith, *Single and Feeling Good*, 14.

Two

The Most Unpopular Requirement for Marriage

While the good-time atmosphere of a roller skating party provided the setting for our first romantically inclined encounter, the door to our relationship actually started to open sometime before that in an entirely different setting: a prayer meeting.

L   Throughout high school I was active in the music ministry of Youth For Christ, a parachurch youth organization. Shortly before I graduated and left the group, a newcomer joined. He provided a much-needed musical addition to the group, but beyond that, we veterans didn't know much about him. What was he like? Why did he join? What were his motives? How seriously did he take his faith? He was a jock, obviously; beyond that, who was Bill Hybels?

He showed up on Tuesday night when the group gathered for prayer in the basement of our YFC director's home. We had planned a series of concerts in local churches; we desperately wanted people to be drawn closer to the Lord through our music and spoken words, so we earnestly prayed to that end. One by one, we went around the circle of folding chairs.

When Bill prayed, it became obvious why he was there. He truly loved God and had a passion for people who didn't know Him or who related to Him only on a surface level. He believed that music had the power to move people, and though he considered himself only minimally gifted musically, he wanted to do what he could. He wanted to be part of a difference-making team.

L Years later, when Bill and I were youth leaders, we witnessed again and again the abandon with which high school students throw themselves and their emotions into whatever they do. That night, in the spring of 1969, we were ourselves caught up in that youthful abandonment of emotion. For those brief moments we were single-minded, we were totally devoted, we were purely motivated. We felt, together with the rest of the team, united in an ultimately worthy cause—we were giving ourselves to something greater than ourselves, something beyond ourselves, something infinitely important.

After the meeting, I headed for my car with a lingering awareness of what mattered most in life. I walked past Bill's truck just as he slammed the door, but then he opened it and caught my attention.

"I've followed your involvement in the Junior Miss Pageant. I really respect how open you've been about your faith. It took guts for you to play a Christian song for the talent competition. The whole community knows that you're serious about what you believe."

We talked about my reasons for entering the pageant, about why we were each committed to YFC, about the Christian camp in Wisconsin where he counseled every summer, about my family's summer plans to work at a mission station in the jungle of Ecuador.

It was just a friendly conversation; at that time, we were both happily dating other people. But there was an obvious spiritual connection that came back to "haunt" us later. You see, while both of us had dated a number of sincere, dedicated Christians, for some reason neither of us had ever sensed the degree of spiritual compatibility that we sensed with one another. When we eventually did begin dating, this obvious compatibility was of paramount importance. Neither of us felt responsible for the other's spiritual growth. Neither of us had to try to lure the other into greater devotion to Christ. In the natural course of our conversations we challenged one another to deeper commitment. As I confessed sin in my life it awakened Bill's awareness to sin in his life. As he shared personal insights

L from Scripture it encouraged me to search out insights of my own.

It is true that our spiritual compatibility, as strong as it is and always has been, did not assure us an easy marriage. I can say, however, with no exaggeration, that it has saved our marriage. I believe with every fiber of my being that had either of us been less submitted to Jesus Christ than we were, we could not have surmounted the challenges that our marriage has presented. We have both had to change so much—from the inside out—and only the indwelling Holy Spirit could have brought about such changes. We have both had to say "I'm sorry" so many times, and only the chastening of a Perfect Father could have humbled us enough to repeat those words—again. We have both faced overwhelming external pressures because of the visibility of our ministry, and only a vital, daily connection with the All-powerful One could have given us the strength to stand firm. We have both known heart-wrenching griefs and disappointments, and only solitary, late-night vigils in the presence of the God of Comfort could have brought us through.

All along the way we have needed—yes, *needed!*—to have our combined humanness divinely reshaped and empowered and embraced.

We both believe in every word and principle presented in this book. Marriage is a complex affair that must be viewed from many perspectives and built up with a variety of tools. But it all starts here, with spiritual compatibility. So don't skim this chapter. Don't gloss this issue. Determine now to base your relationship on something you can build a future on.

THE BUYING MOOD

Auto industry insiders know that most car buyers purchase cars within forty-eight hours of walking into the first showroom. That is why dealers display new cars so seductively in their showrooms, and why salespeople try so hard to seal the deal fast. They know that after forty-eight hours the "mood" will likely wear off. The customer will return to reality and allow good judgment to prevail.

But before that happens, it is a passionate game of impulse and action. People in the buying mood often get fascinated with—even fixate on—a single feature of a car they are considering. Sometimes they actually buy the car because of that one feature. It may be the sleek design of the dashboard. Or the bells and whistles that make them feel like they are in an airplane cockpit. Sometimes it is the mag wheels and raised-letter tires. Or the leather interior. Often it is the sound system; they sit in the car for ten minutes singing along with the radio, then get out and sign on the dotted line.

People in the buying mood seldom read consumer reports, check repair records, or analyze how quickly various models depreciate. Few even check the warranty data. They are in the mood. They are fired up. Better judgment has been temporarily suspended, so they make the deal, sign the papers, and drive their shiny new toy home—all within forty-eight hours.

But what happens to many of those people two or three days later, when the shine wears off and a payment book as big as their Bibles arrives in the mail? Second thoughts? Buyer's remorse?

But wait, you say, *it's only a car—ten or fifteen thousand dollars—maybe twenty. Nobody would be that careless about a really important decision.*

Read what a real estate agent said about the house-buying mood. "It's real, all right. That's why we try to move so fast. If you don't get 'em to sign a contract within a day or two, you lose 'em. That mood doesn't last long, and when it passes, it's all over.

"But when they're in the mood," he continued, "it's unbelievable. A woman will buy a house because she loves the laundry room. A man will walk into the garage and envision where his workshop will be, and it's a done deal. They don't check the heating system, the plumbing, the electrical, the attic, the basement. If they are in the buying mood, they work fast. They sign."

Don't you wonder how many of those buyers end up regretting their emotional decisions? Or wishing they had waited for sound judgment to return before they signed on for a six-figure commitment?

Still, you say, *it's only a house. No one would ever make such a careless decision about something really important. Say, a lifetime partner. No one would be foolish enough to fixate on one or two features of another person without carefully scrutinizing other qualities, or to get engaged and set a wedding date while their judgment was held hostage by hormones. No one would do that. Would they?*

Would they? Unfortunately, too often they would. You see, there *is* a *marrying mood*—a marrying mood that causes temporary insanity and sabotages normally clear-thinking brains. And too many single adults, young and old, get caught up in it.

The wrong car? You can trade it in. The wrong house? You can sell it. The wrong spouse?

UNWELCOME ADVICE

People in the car-buying mood hate it when interested friends say, "But I read in *Car and Driver* . . ." People in the house-buying mood hate it when well-meaning neighbors say, "But I heard from my friend who's a builder . . ." And people in the marrying mood *really* hate it when concerned pastors say, "But the Bible says . . ."

They especially hate it when those pastors turn to the infamous passage where Paul gives the first requirement for meaningful, God-honoring marriage. "Do not be yoked together with unbelievers," he says. "For what do righteousness and wickedness have in common? Or what fellowship can light have with darkness? What harmony is there between Christ and Belial? What does a believer have in common with an unbeliever?" (2 Cor. 6:14–15).

That is one of the least appreciated verses in Scripture. Some singles claim it sounds downright discriminatory—a kind of spiritual apartheid: The white hats can't mix with the black hats; God's children are too good to marry unbelievers. Others argue that it hurts evangelism: "How can we win unbelievers to the Lord if we can't date them and 'love 'em' into the kingdom?" It is amazing how much disobedience flourishes under the guise of evangelism.

But these questioning singles do have an understandable complaint. The call for spiritual compatibility *does reduce the field*. In fact, for many singles it pares the number of eligible candidates down to a mere handful.

Still, we have grown weary of hearing God take a bad rap for this passage. Weary of people trusting God with every area of their lives except this one. Weary of people ignoring this passage. Distorting it. Justifying disobeying it: *He's almost a believer; she says she'll become a believer after we're married*. Above all, we are weary of dealing with the consequences people face when they make statements like that, and then end up with a spiritually *in*compatible spouse.

A COMMON TREASURE

In this chapter we want to argue God's case by presenting some possible reasons why He calls Christians to spiritual compatibility in marriage. We hope it will become clear that there is nothing discriminatory, capricious, or cruel about 2 Corinthians 6:14. It is, on the contrary, the loving plea of a Father who is gracious, tenderhearted, and protective of His children.

The first probable reason for demanding spiritual compatibility is to ensure that marriage partners will share a common treasure, to make sure that every husband and wife can share that which is most precious to them with their spouse. If you think this isn't important, consider what it is like to have to keep *anything* you love—even something of a purely temporal nature—to yourself.

B   My favorite recreation is ocean sailing. I can't begin to explain how much I enjoy the motion of the swells, the sound of the waves, the feel of the spray, the power of the wind. I wish I loved something like chess, or gardening—something less expensive, something I could do more often. But I can't help it. I *love* ocean sailing.

Not long ago I took five men from my church—a friend, two board members, an elder, and a staff member—ocean sailing for a week. Most of them had never been ocean sailing, so I couldn't wait to get them on the boat. I knew it would be the highlight of their lives.

B   The first day out of the harbor was a sailor's dream: twenty-five-knot winds, clear sky, six- to eight-foot seas. We headed out to open water. A couple hours out, I was standing at the helm singing at the top of my lungs—laughing, joking, having the time of my life. All of a sudden I realized that no one was joking back. No one was laughing or joining in song. So I tried to cheer them up. "Does it get any better than this?" I shouted. "Are we having fun, or what?"

No response. In fact, I noticed that some of the guys were looking a little green. A couple of them headed down below to "rest." Our navigator took the charts and disappeared—for the rest of the day. The other two guys situated themselves near the rails, and all I can say is that they both experienced "unplanned protein spills." I sat at the helm with one guy hanging over the rail on one side of me, and another guy over the rail on the opposite side. I tried to maintain my euphoria at sea, but with no one to share it, it faded. So, with a perfect wind still blowing, I headed back toward protected waters.

As much as I love ocean sailing, it is no match for how I feel about my relationship with Jesus Christ: After seven days of sailing I've had my fill; I don't think about it for another six months. But I never get my fill of growing as a Christian. I don't get tired of learning about the Lord or talking to Him. I don't get tired of teaching my kids about Him or worshiping Him.

My wife doesn't get excited about a lot of the things I enjoy. She is not big on Harley-Davidson motorcycles or twin-engine airplanes or high-performance race cars. And though she enjoys ocean sailing, it is not the thrill for her that it is for me. But she loves Christ with a passion every bit as strong as mine. We can discuss together lessons we have learned in our personal Bible study. We can tell each other about answers to prayer. We can trade information we have found in Christian books. We can take long walks and dream together about what God can do through us. We can encourage one another to commit more of ourselves to God. We can talk openly about sin in our lives and challenge one another to greater obedience.

B It would be torture for me not to be able to share the greatest treasure in my life with my wife. And that is nothing unique to me. To have a spouse yawn about that which means more than anything else in life would bring heartache to any true believer.

When a person comes into a personal relationship with Jesus Christ, Jesus becomes not only his answer to life's complexities, but also his Savior, his Friend, and ultimately, his Treasure. He realizes that he has been forgiven, cleansed, and liberated, and he stands in awe of the wonder of it all. He begins to think about the Lord throughout the day. He finds himself singing worship songs in the car. He looks forward to going to church. Eventually he catches himself talking about Him in enthusiastic tones to whomever will listen. He doesn't make himself do that. It happens naturally because such an important dimension of his life cries out to be shared with friends, acquaintances, neighbors, family members—and especially, his spouse.

God loves His children so much that He wants to spare them the pain of having an unshared treasure. So He says, "Throw romance out the window for a while. Put sexual excitement on the back burner. Look at the long haul. What you need to look for first is a spouse with whom you can share Me. A spouse with whom you can share your Greatest Treasure."

There are scores of godly men and women in our church married to unbelievers. Many of them became Christians after they married. Others were Christians when they married, but they disobeyed this passage. After an evening of moving corporate worship, one such woman said, "Do you know what it's like to go home after a service like this and be so filled with the grace of God that you think you're going to explode—but you can't share that with your husband? It's awful. God has forgiven me for my disobedience, but every day I live with the pain of the mistake I made years ago." That woman hangs on to the hope that someday her husband will be influenced by her example and become a Christian. But he is no puppet on a string; she has no guarantee. So she waits and carries the pain.

That is the pain God wants to help us avoid. Is that so unreasonable? Is it capricious or cruel?

A COMMON BLUEPRINT

The second probable reason God insists on spiritual compatibility is to enable spouses to build their marriage from a common blueprint. Imagine the frustration of two carpenters trying to build a house with two different sets of plans. With conflicting designs, conflicting dimensions, and conflicting materials, the effort would be doomed. Even a casual observer would see the futility of the project. "You can't build a house from different blueprints," he'd say. "It won't work!"

The same can be said to naive lovers who enter marriage with totally different plans for how to build their relationship. She has *her* set of plans based on her background, her parents' marriage, and her world and life view. He has *his* set of plans based on his background, his parents' marriage, and his world and life view. Soon those individual blueprints are expressed in verbal form.

"A decent husband would act this way."

"A decent wife should be seen and not heard."

"Only a mental pygmy would make a statement like that."

"Well, you're looking up at me!"

And on it goes.

God's plan is to step into a messy situation like that and take the faulty plans, crumple them up, and throw them away. Then He says, "Here, take My blueprint—both of you. In the Bible I have outlined in great detail how marriages should be built. I have stated clearly what it will take for you to be a godly wife, and you to be a godly husband. I have provided plans for handling anger. Plans for conflict resolution. Plans for how to encourage and love and inspire one another. Plans for how to serve one another. Plans for how to compromise. It's the perfect blueprint, so use it! Share it! Obey it! You can't build a successful marriage without it."

It is safe to say that ninety percent of the snits we have had in our marriage have resulted from one or both of us inflicting our individual blueprints on the other, or simply disobeying God's blueprint. Fortunately, because we share a common Lord and both ultimately trust His blueprint, when our feelings subside and we regain our wits, we turn to Him. We take our Bibles, head for our respective corners, and spend a few minutes reminding ourselves of His plan. Then we come back together ready to move ahead constructively.

Many people wonder about the high divorce rate in the U.S. We wonder why it isn't higher. What can couples expect when they refuse to trade in their individual blueprints for God's?

A COMMON STRENGTH

In this imperfect world there is trouble, evil, heartache, pain, disappointment, illness, loss, and grief. There are financial setbacks, emotional upheavals, automobile accidents, barren wombs, and deaths of loved ones. The list of possible trials and tribulations goes on and on. No individual or married couple goes through life without being marked by the residual effects of the fallenness of man. Rogue winds will blow through every marriage from time to time.

The third reason God calls for spiritual compatibility in marriage is so both spouses can, through prayer, tap into a common strength in the face of these inevitable adversities.

God doesn't want one partner turning to pills or chemicals or bottles. He doesn't want one partner escaping reality in a stranger's bed. He doesn't want one partner screaming, "I can't take it anymore. I give up. I quit."

One woman said, "My husband has gone numb. He won't talk. He won't share his feelings with me. He won't spend time with our daughters. He won't make love to me. Our son died, and now he's dying inside. I tell him to pray. I tell him to turn to Christ. But he won't listen. I can't reach him. I can't reach him!"

What a difference it makes in a marriage when both partners can turn to God and find that He is "a refuge and strength, a present help in time of need." It frees each spouse from having to wonder how the other will handle the upsets in life.

B   Some time ago Lynne was facing a deadline with a book
}   she was editing. I walked into her office one morning and
}   saw the manuscript thrown all over the floor. She had been
}   working through the night, and it was obvious the night

B had not gone well. I knew there was not much I could do, but I offered to help. "No, no," she said. "It'll be okay." She grabbed the journal where she records her prayers and went out on the back porch.

About an hour later she came back in. "I'm okay now. I just had to put this whole thing back into perspective and trust God. I know He'll give me the strength to finish this if I just keep turning to Him."

I thought, *Whew! Am I glad this woman has access to supernatural strength.* I have seen her bounce back from two midterm miscarriages and the loss of loved ones. I have seen her persevere through challenges. I have seen her face extremely intimidating situations. I am so thankful that she knows where to turn when life gets tough.

How different our lives would be if either of us had access only to human strength. How frustrating it would be for one of us to watch the other sink into the abyss of despair, or to disintegrate inside when supernatural assistance is only a prayer away. The ability to tap into God's strength is a gift spouses give to one another.

L When Bill's father died, I knew how deeply he grieved, but I didn't have to wonder whether he would "pull out of it." When he has faced unusual pressures in the ministry, I have not had to worry that he would crumble under them. When I have seen him face-down on the living room floor, agonizing over difficult decisions, I have not had to question the outcome. I know that in prayer he can receive the comfort, the energy, the direction he needs.

Some time ago a young couple in our church found out that their beautiful, outgoing, energetic ten-year-old daughter has an inoperable brain tumor. There is absolutely nothing they can do for her. One of their closest friends said, "In the midst of their excruciating pain they are living out the kind of faith the rest of us talk about." Why are they able to do that? Because as individuals they have learned how to tap God's strength. And in the middle of this agony they bring that divine strength to one another, share it, and in it find the will and the courage to go on. What a tragedy if only one of them knew how to tap God's comfort and power; their foundation would be only half as secure.

Every marriage will sometime be sucked into the swirling center of life's storm. When that happens, God wants both partners to be able to reach out to Him for strength and help.

COMMON VALUES

There has never been an age like the one we are living in. This is the age of nuclear war, of me-ism, of relativism, of abortion on demand, of promiscuity. It is an age when adults lure children into sexual acts and drugs are distributed in grade schools. It is an age of confusion and conflict—especially for children.

The fourth reason God insists on spiritual compatibility in marriage is so children can be raised by parents who share common values. This is no time for little Bobby to have to wonder why Mommy says Jesus Christ is the Way, the Truth, and the Life, while Daddy uses His name as a curse word. This is no time for little Mary to be set adrift by space-age parents who can't themselves agree on values, so they proudly announce that she can tread water indefinitely on the seas of relativism. This is *not* what contemporary kids need.

This is a time for children to see a united front. This is a time for parents to clarify values and educate their children morally and spiritually. This is a time for both moms and dads to teach the truth, model the truth, enforce the truth, and love their children into the truth.

There is a cruel, ungodly world out there that wants to eat our kids for lunch. Our son was offered drugs when he was ten years old and taunted by friends to "have sex" with a fourth grade girl. In the halls of her suburban high school our daughter is daily bombarded with profanity and sexual innuendo, with immoral lifestyles and alluring temptations. Never before have our children and yours so needed the advantage of being led by parents with shared values and beliefs; there is power in a united front. But you can't fake that. Kids pick up on the discrepancies. So, what do they do when they sense that the two primary authority figures in their lives don't agree on the basics? What do they believe? What do they have to go on? What can they grab on to and say, "This must be true"? How can they determine right from wrong?

The only way to present a united front is to marry someone who has the same Lord—someone who cherishes the same treasure, trusts the same blueprint, and taps the same strength. Only then can you share the same values and establish a home where children can get the kind of guidance they need. We love our kids more than we ever dreamed we could love anyone. It would break our hearts if every time one of us left for work or traveled for a few days we had to wonder what the other parent was teaching them. What must it be like to wonder what values your spouse is passing on while you are away? Or to fear that they are contradicting what you have said? Or to hear them openly questioning the beliefs you have tried to instill?

A COURAGEOUS DECISION

Second Corinthians 6:14 is not discrimination; it is not capriciousness. It is sovereign wisdom. It is for our good. It is for the future welfare of every unmarried person. It is God's protective love expressed in practical form. Still, we know the implications are frightening for some single people reading this book. Some of you are all wrapped up romantically with a person who doesn't share your faith. What do you do now? We hope you will end the relationship. We don't say that lightly because we know it won't be easy. But is there a better choice? Look to the future. Do you want a lifetime of pain and frustration?

Once a month the elders of our church meet with people who are sick or grieving or needy in some other way. One month a woman in her mid-twenties sat in a group and wept quietly until it was her turn to share. "I've been dating a guy who's not a Christian," she stammered. "After Bill's message on spiritual compatibility I knew I had to break up with him and I did. But it's so hard. I really loved him. I know that someday I'll be glad I did this, but right now it just hurts so much. Please pray for me." The next month she was back. She still missed him; she still grieved her broken dreams. But she said, "I know it was right. I know God will bless this decision. I'm not sorry I did it."

God can give you the courage that young woman had. If you are in a romantic relationship with an unbeliever, or if you sense a friendship might be heading that way, draw on His power to help you get out, call it off, make a break. Then surround yourself with people who can pray for you, encourage you, and cheer you on. If you choose to disobey God in this, you are on your own and you are headed for disaster. But if you obey, if you make the hard choice, if you trust His Word, you will find yourself on the road to peace and blessing.

SYNCHRONIZED

One of the tricks in learning to fly a twin-engine airplane is getting both engines synchronized properly. If one engine is just slightly overpowered the plane will vibrate and veer off to one side. It takes careful attention to the gauges and an educated ear to determine—and hear—which engine needs to be adjusted.

B When I first began working on my multiengine rating, I got very frustrated when I felt that slight vibration that signaled the need to advance or retard an engine. *Which one do I adjust? How much?* It was such a great feeling to finally get to the point where I didn't have to agonize so much over every adjustment. Eventually it became second nature. I could just put my hands on the controls and feel it. It was so exhilarating to come in for landing with both engines synchronized perfectly. It felt so . . . right.

That feeling of *rightness*—of being perfectly synchronized—is why God insists on Christians marrying only other Christians. He wants spouses to be finely adjusted to one another. He wants them to be equally powered. He wants them to share the same sensitivity to the will of God. He wants their ears to be equally tuned to the leading of the Spirit.

That kind of synchronization implies more than just a shared belief. True spiritual compatibility implies a shared *intensity* of belief, a shared degree of commitment. In other words, a vibrant, Spirit-led, radically committed Christian woman should never settle for a nominal, comfortable Christian man who does little more than wear the lapel pin and mimic the jargon. What happens when the Spirit leads her to sacrifice time or money, or go out on the limb of faith, or change careers, or churches, or lifestyles? What happens when she wants to obey that leading, but her less committed spouse says, "Don't get fanatical. Why do you have to make waves? I don't like crawling out on limbs. I like our life just the way it is. No changes." That response spells major trouble and disappointment for the deeply committed spouse.

B As I look back over the years I see how absolutely crucial it was for me to have a spouse who was passionately devoted to Jesus Christ. Shortly after Lynne and I were married, I sensed God calling me to leave our successful youth ministry and start a church with no people, no building, and no money. It was clearly a "divine demotion." It meant sacrifice, loss of security, reduced salary, increased challenge, and harder work. When I told Lynne about it, she said, "I'll pray about it." A few days later she came back and said, "You're right. He's calling. Let's go."

At other times, we have felt led to give away possessions or money. Every time we have sought God's direction, we have been able to agree on the right plan or the exact amount. When we have had to make housing changes or education decisions for our children, our individual prayers have led us to compatible conclusions. When we have had scheduling conflicts, we have been able to resolve the issues by submitting to the wisdom we've each received from God.

That is synchronization. That is being equally yoked. That is the kind of spiritual oneness God longs for all married people to enjoy.

Three

Character, Phone Bills, and Chemistry

B Romance was never my strong suit. I proposed to Lynne in her parents' garage; I took my Harley-Davidson on our honeymoon; I thought our best anniversary was the one we spent watching a video of *Rocky III*. But several years into our marriage, I realized that being a godly husband meant more than bringing home a paycheck and occasionally talking shop with Lynne. I had to grow in the gentle art of romance.

So for starters, I figured that meant flowers. Beyond that, I didn't have a clue, but I knew I could get the flower job done. As confirmation from God that I was moving in the right direction, who do you think set up shop out of the trunk of his '58 DeSoto at the corner opposite our church? The flower man!

So, quite regularly, on my way home from work or from meetings, I would pull over to the side of the road, buy a bundle of roses or carnations from the flower man, and take them home to Lynne. *What a husband!* I thought as I handed over my three bucks. *Hundreds of men drive right by this intersection past the flower man, but do they buy flowers for their wives? No. But do I? Certainly.* I remember looking at all those other insensitive men and thinking, *How do they do it? How do they pass up an opportunity like this?*

Yet when I proudly presented these flowers to Lynne, fully expecting her to hire the Marine Corps Band to play "Hail to the Chief," her response was rather lukewarm.

"Gee thanks," she said. "Where'd you get these?"

"Where else? My buddy the flower man—you know, the guy with the '58 DeSoto at Barrington and Algonquin. I'm a volume buyer now. Because I stop there so often he gives

B me a buck off, and if they're a little wilted, he gives me two bucks off. I figure they'll perk up when you put 'em in water."

"Of course," she said.

I did that regularly for quite some time—until Lynne's lack of enthusiasm for the gift drained my enthusiasm for the practice. I'd leave church, see the flower man, be tempted to stop, then think, *No way. I hate being taken for granted.* So I'd wave, he'd wave, and I'd go home without flowers.

Some time later, on our regularly scheduled date night, Lynne and I decided to clear the air on anything that might be bothering either of us. We do that now and then. We sit down in a cheap restaurant (not only am I unromantic, I'm also Dutch) and say, "What's going on? Is there anything we need to talk about? Is there anything amiss in our relationship?" On that particular night, Lynne took out her list and started checking off items, and I said, "Ooooh, you're right on that one. Sorry. Eeeh, that one too. Yep. Guilty as charged. Guilty. Guilty. You're right again." She ended her list, and I was in a pile. I said, "I really am sorry. But trust me. I'm going to do better."

She said, "Now, what about you?" I really didn't have any complaints, but after hearing her grocery list, I thought I should say *something*. I scrambled. "Well, I do have one little problem. Have you noticed the absence of flowers lately?"

"No," she said. "I haven't really paid attention." *How could she say that?*

"We have a problem. I can't figure it out. Hundreds of thousands of husbands pass by that corner. Do *they* stop for flowers? No! Do I stop? Yes! Do you play 'Hail to the Chief' when I get home? No! What gives? What's your problem?"

Her answer made my head spin. She looked me straight in the eyes and quietly said, "The truth is, Bill, I'm not too impressed when you give me half-dead flowers that came out of the trunk of a '58 DeSoto that you were lucky enough to run into on your way home from work. The flowers are cheap and the effort is minimal. The way I see

B it, you're not investing enough time or energy to warrant a wholehearted response from me. You're not thinking about what would make me happy; you're just doing what's convenient for you."

I said, "Okay, let's get this straight. You would be happier if I got up from my desk in the middle of my busy day, threw my study schedule to the wind, walked all the way across the parking lot, got in my car, and made a special trip to Barrington where I'd have to pay quadruple the price just because it said Barrington on the bag? And you wouldn't mind if the extra time that took would crimp my workout schedule at the Y? (Remember, Lynne, high blood pressure and heart disease run in my family.) And you wouldn't mind if I came home late because of *all* the extra running around I'd have to do to get you *expensive* flowers? Is *that* what you're telling me? *That* would make you happy?"

I was proud of myself. I missed my calling. I should have been a lawyer. The jury would have been spellbound. They would have been thoroughly convinced.

Without batting an eyelash, Lynne said, "Yes, that would make me happy."

I couldn't believe it! "What're you talking about? What you're asking for is neither practical, economical, nor an efficient use of time."

"That's a great definition of romance, Bill. You're learning!"

Why do we share this story with you? Because things like this happen in marriage all the time. It's one thing after the other. Sometimes we wonder how anybody survives this institution. It rattles your thinking. It turns your expectations inside out. It stretches you to the breaking point—then pushes you a little further. It's true! Living intimately with another human being is the greatest challenge in the world. We're nearing the end of two decades of marriage, and we still marvel at all that is required to build and nurture a relationship with a spouse.

There have been times, in fact, when we have even questioned our wisdom in choosing one another. Sometimes the difficult eras have lasted so long, the issues have been so hard to work through, and our confrontations have been so painful. But always, after we have finally resolved the tension, we have been able to recite a long list of concrete reasons why we know we are well-suited for one another. Being able to do that has been so important. It has given us the motivation to struggle over whatever hurdles we have faced. It has given us the hope to say, "There's a light at the end of this tunnel. If we keep working, we're going to end up with something great. It's going to be worth the effort."

CHECKLIST

Life in an imperfect world throws enough obstacles and curve balls to make marriage with even an ideal spouse hard to handle. Imagine what it is like to face those challenges with someone who you realize was not a suitable person for you to marry. Again, the most miserable people in the world are not single people who wish they were married, but rather, married people who realize that their marriage was a mistake. By God's grace, even marriages like that can often be renewed and saved. But it takes a staggering amount of work.

That is why single people cannot afford to ride a toboggan slide of emotion into marriage. They *must* go through a careful premarital checklist that starts with spiritual compatibility. They *must* spend enough time dating to make sure they share a common treasure, a common blueprint, a common strength, and common values.

But even that is not enough. After a message on spiritual compatibility a young woman said, "So, the point is that I just need to identify a sincere, dedicated believer, and then go for it. Right? I mean, as long as he's a true Christian, I can't go far wrong. Right?" Wrong. A marriage between two believers can be a disaster. Just because two people are right with God doesn't mean they are right for each other. Each of us could have been miserably married to a number of very godly people. As much as we value our spiritual compatibility, it is not the *only* reason we chose one another.

WORTHY OF RESPECT

"I love Beth. I'm just not sure I like her very much!" The young man laughed as he described his latest marital conflict, but it seemed to be a nervous laughter. Perhaps there was more truth in his words than humor.

"It's a good thing we're 'in love.' I don't think we'd make it as friends!" *Why not?* one wonders. *And what will happen when these naive lovers find out that marriage is more about friendship than about being "in love"?*

Relationships can weather thunderstorms and gale-force winds as long as there is one very important element present: respect. That starts, of course, with being able to respect someone spiritually, but it goes beyond that. It means respecting the other person on the sheer merits of his or her basic character.

Just for a moment, put aside the spiritual dimension of life. What respectable character traits do you see in your potential spouse? Do you respect his maturity level? His decision-making ability? His priorities? His degree of self-discipline? Do you respect her commitment to her vocation? Her consistency? Her loyalty? Her relational patterns? Can you look at your potential spouse and say, "I truly admire this person. There are so many things I like, and I keep finding more. This person has integrity and character. Even if we weren't dating, I would like to be friends." That is a sign of healthy character compatibility.

BEST BEHAVIOR

Unfortunately, the contemporary American courtship system does not give dating couples much opportunity to test character compatibility, because it ensures that dating partners will see each other only at their best. They get all dressed up and follow a well-thought-out itinerary: They go to a concert, a movie, or a play. They go out for dinner. They sit in the driveway and talk. Then they part ways and wait for the next well-planned function. It may be fun and exciting, but a steady schedule of plastic, programmed encounters is a poor way to detect character and an unrealistic way for young couples to prepare for marriage. There may be glamour and drama and excitement, but what are they learning about one another? What is really happening in their relationship?

B When Lynne and I started dating, we took another approach. It may have had more to do with me being cheap and busy than being wise, but the end result was to our benefit. I would arrive at Lynne's house after working at the farm and say, "I have to go back and put the equipment away. Why don't you come and 'hang around' while I do that?" Sometimes on our dates I would have to drive a semi from Kalamazoo to Michigan's upper peninsula to pick up a load of potatoes. Lynne would ride in the truck with me—twelve hours, round trip. What do you do while you are cleaning farm equipment and riding in produce trucks? You talk. You discuss your life histories. You share your dreams about the future. You find out how much you really have in common. You learn what the other person values. You discover what it is like to share the mundane with one another.

That is, after all, what marriage is. It is sharing the mundane together. It is going through the daily routine of life. Of course, there are exceptions: Nights out on the town. Occasional vacations. Peak experiences. But most of marriage is lived in the mundane—where you see each other for who you really are, where you look reality in the face. You sure better like what you see. You better respect the man or woman who sits across the table from you every night and wakes up in your bed every morning.

EVERYTHING'S FINE NOW

In a recent poll, people were asked what character defect they are least able to tolerate in others. What topped the list? Dishonesty.

"I can't stand it when someone says one thing, then does something else."

"I hate it when people deceive me."

"I can't tolerate people who lie."

Clearly, dishonesty in relationships is public enemy number one.

Not long ago a young woman from our church told us happily that she was in a serious dating relationship, then soberly added, "But we had a little trouble recently. I found out he was seeing someone else on the side. I felt terrible. He stopped seeing her, though, and we've worked it all out. Everything's fine now."

It seemed to us that things were "fine now" a little too quickly, so we probed. "How long had he been seeing her?" She said she didn't know; she hadn't asked. "You didn't ask?! You didn't find out how long he had been deceiving you? This is a major issue you're talking about. You should read him the riot act! If he deceives you during the courtship phase, what do you think is going to happen during marriage? Is a leopard going to change its spots just because it takes a trip to the marriage altar? You better find out what this guy is really like."

"I guess I've been afraid to find out," she said.

Unfortunately, that is too often the problem. Many people choose to ignore the truth rather than risk finding out that their potential mate's character is less than shining. But the truth always comes out eventually. So ask the tough questions before it is too late. Is this person careless with the truth? Does he tell white lies? Exaggerate? Does she make use of subtle distortions? Do you sometimes sense that you haven't heard the whole story?

Ephesians 4:25 says, "Therefore each of you must put off falsehood and speak truthfully to his neighbor, for we are all members of one body." There is no room in godly character for dishonesty. There should be no tolerance of the slightest form of deceit in a potential marriage partner. Can you imagine having to go through life wondering what was *really* in the checking account? Who your husband was *really* having dinner with? Where your wife was *really* going?

BEWARE OF BLOCKAGE

Another good indicator of people's character is their sense of responsibility.

A recently engaged man explained why he loved his fiancée

so much. "She's a free spirit," he said. "She's unpredictable. She's spontaneous and carefree. She's one surprise after the next. It's fun just to be around her!" Several months later, having just called off their wedding, he said, "She drove me absolutely crazy. She was spacey, undisciplined, careless, irresponsible. She ran the car out of gas, bounced checks, went on unplanned shopping sprees. And to think I almost married her. Who knows what would have happened!"

Here's a comment we have heard more than once: "I love him so much. And he's so talented. I know he'll sell his paintings someday. He's also going to do some sketching and write poetry for a living." Six months later she's bemoaning the fact that "the freeloader won't find a real job!"

Why is it that people who are courting describe their potential spouses with phrases like "charming idiosyncrasies" and "delightfully spontaneous," when what they really ought to call them is *irresponsible*? It is because of what psychologists call *blockage,* which is the tendency to block out reality because of the excitement of being in love.

A counselor friend of ours described how she had been the victim of blockage. "I'm a very neat person. When I went to my future husband's apartment, I would walk ankle deep in socks and underwear and sweatpants, and there would be pizza cartons and pop cans scattered all over. I would look at that mess and laugh, but it never dawned on me that that mess was going to come into my house. It never dawned on me." Her husband said, "I had the same kind of blockage. It never dawned on me that I would have to clean up my act in order to live in peace with her." He never dreamed it would have to change and she never dreamed it wouldn't.

Some time ago we talked to a divorced woman who had gotten fed up with her former husband's constant mismanagement of money; it finally destroyed their marriage. We learned recently that this same woman has fallen madly in love with a man who hasn't been consistently employed in ten years and is deeply in debt. She plans to marry him. When confronted about it, she said, "But he's a Christian; he loves the Lord." Though no one denies that, the fact is, he is a very unfinished product with serious character issues to work on.

Blockage. It happens and it is dangerous. The only way to

avoid it is to be ruthlessly analytical regarding your future spouse. How responsible is this person vocationally? Does he jump from job to job? Is she conscientious and dependable? How responsible is this person relationally? Is he loyal to his friends? Have her friendships stood the test of time? What about finances? Does she have a budget and save for the future? Does he pay his bills on time? What about physically? Does she take care of her health? Does he keep his body in shape? Or domestically? Does she maintain her possessions reasonably well? Is he adequately organized? Or legally? Does she cut legal corners? Does he joke that laws are made to be broken?

If these questions strike you as a shade too picky, beware. What looks like a slight flaw from the relative distance of courtship may be revealed as a major disfigurement from the up-close perspective of marriage. Disappointments that can be tolerated nicely during a weekly date may become intolerable when faced on a daily basis. *No* question is too petty to ask. *No* concern is too insignificant to raise.

Jesus said, "Be shrewed as snakes and as innocent as doves" (Matt. 10:16). For dating couples that means, *Don't lose your street smarts. Don't put your brains on hold. Don't get so emotionally involved that you forget to ask the tough questions. Don't turn your head to little deceptions, white lies, slight irresponsibilities.* If you do that now, you'll pay later.

Do you respect your future spouse's character enough to live with it for a lifetime?

KEEP IT FRESH

Depth of character manifests itself in high degrees of honesty and responsibility, and also in an intangible quality we call the *vitality quotient*. The vitality quotient is what keeps the mundane from turning to boredom. While it is seldom talked about, it is critical to a healthy marriage.

Experts agree that boredom kills many a marriage. During the courtship phase, life is exciting. In the marketplace, life is stimulating. On vacations, life is fun. But at home life easily becomes a series of boring routines. Cooking. Cleaning. Laundry. TV. Lawn care. Car pools. Washing dishes. TV. Answering mail. Shopping. Running errands. TV. Taking out the garbage. Washing the car. Painting the hallway. TV. That's what it's like on the practical plains of reality, and it can sap the life out of a marriage . . . unless partners tenaciously refuse to let the routine sterilize them, unless they refuse to become boring people, unless they determine to keep growing and exploring and learning.

People with depth of character seek new levels of spiritual maturity that bring about positive change. They pursue marketplace challenges that force them to increase their skills. They try new recreational activities that push their physical limits. They expand their horizons relationally. They experiment romantically. And that keeps a relationship fresh, even in the midst of the mundane.

B One thing I love about Lynne is that she is a vital person; she has a wide range of interests and skills. Her primary passions are reading and writing, so she loves to talk about literature and authors and words and ideas—but she is hardly a stereotypical bookworm. She runs, does aerobics, wind-surfs, sails, snow skis, and at age thirty-eight she learned how to water ski barefoot! She enjoys music from classical to rock and is an accomplished flutist. Several years ago, I came home from a meeting and heard a horrible noise coming out of the study—it sounded like a wounded animal. I ran in and found Lynne playing the oboe. "I just had my first lesson," she explained. She was experimenting again, growing, stretching.

Take a critical look at the person you are considering marrying. What are his interests? What does she get excited about? Is he open to new adventures? Does she come up with fresh ideas? If you see a person who lacks energy, who is content with a narrow world, who disdains change—*be careful!* A lifetime is a long time to be bored.

PHONE BILLS

"Trust us. We talk. We know how to communicate. We should be stockholders in AT & T! We even fax love poems to each other at work. We nearly asphyxiate ourselves every other night, talking in the car in the driveway. We communicate!"

Most couples think they have a lock on the third important requirement for successful marriage: communicational compatibility. "We talk," they say. "We talk a lot." But the issue here is not quantity, but rather quality—depth of communication, vulnerability, exposing secrets, truth-telling and truth-hearing.

B If the issue were quantity, I would win the communication prize—as a trained speaker with a tendency toward extroversion, I spend a lot of time talking. Yet, the biggest hurdle in our marriage has been communication.

Picture this: It is midnight. The full moon is postcard perfect and the breeze is warm. Lynne and I are sitting on a park bench at a wooded camp in Wisconsin. Twenty years old. Dating seriously. No one around. She half faces me, her arms around my shoulders, her head resting against mine. I wrap my arms around her. *This is what it's all about*, I think. Lynne lifts her head and looks deeply into my eyes. "Bill, I just don't feel close to you right now." My mind fills with ways we might get closer, but I refuse to entertain the thoughts. "How can you say you don't feel close to me? For heaven's sake, honey, what do you want?" I hug her a little tighter, laugh off her comment, and dismiss it from my mind.

Big mistake! If I could play that scene over, I would do it this way. I would take her hands off my shoulders, slide about a foot away, look her straight in the eye, and say, "Why don't you feel close to me? What's wrong? What are you feeling? Have I done something to push you away? Have I hurt you? I'll sit here all night to find out why you said that. If you don't know exactly why you said it, just start talking about how you feel. Maybe we can figure it out together."

A response like that would have set a precedent for honest communication that could have made our marriage much easier. Instead we set a precedent for evasiveness, for burying feelings, for dismissing uncomfortable thoughts.

Though honest communication can be difficult and threatening, it is critical to the success of any marriage. Spouses need to know one another intimately. They need to reveal to each other their personal pain, their fears, their failures, their frustrations. They need to speak hard truth to one another and receive it maturely.

Counselors agree that most marriages derail because of inadequate communicatibn. Spouses cannot reach deeper levels of understanding or sustain relational growth if they can't communicate effectively. That is why, when we hear a young man say, "I really love my girlfriend. She's a bit of a mystery to me, but I love her," we want to say, *She shouldn't be a mystery to you! Dig deeper. Find out what she's about.* And that is why we shudder when we hear a young woman say, "I really love him, but he's the strong, silent type. It's hard to know what's going on inside." We have no problem with his strength. But the silent part worries us. Partners have to break through that.

One of the goals of marriage is intimacy—emotional and physical. The key to both is communication. Spouses cannot become soul-mates, nor enjoy the fullness of physical lovemaking, without a deep and accurate knowledge of one another. They can have sexual intercourse without communication, but not the true oneness that flows out of shared feelings, thoughts, frustrations, hopes, and dreams.

Communication is also the key to conflict resolution. Marriage presents even the most compatible couples hundreds—probably thousands—of opportunities for impasse. Each one can chip away at the fragile structure of the union unless both spouses know how to work through disagreements.

Raising healthy children also requires spouses to communicate effectively. Kids need to sit around the dining room table and hear mom and dad talk openly about what is going on in their relationship, in the family, at work. They need to hear feelings and frustrations expressed, discussed, accepted, and sometimes confronted.

When we were dating we both overestimated our communication skills. We assumed that as relatively intelligent, semi-articulate people, we knew everything we had to know about verbally sharing life. So we didn't make communicational growth a priority. We didn't read books or listen to tapes that could have helped us. We just blundered along, creating myriads of misunderstandings that would undermine our relationship years later.

L   I recall many times during our courtship when I sensed that Bill didn't really understand what I meant or how I felt; he didn't grasp what I was trying to say. At those times I should have explained myself again; I should have worked harder to communicate what was inside. But I don't find it easy to express myself verbally; in fact, translating my thoughts into spoken words can be downright exhausting. So, many times I just let the misunderstanding slide. I thought, *Oh well, it's not a big deal. It doesn't really matter*, and I kept quiet. That was a serious mistake. It was a destructive habit that continued long into our marriage and engendered much unnecessary hurt and hostility.

Please learn from our mistakes. The courtship era is the time to get serious about communication. Don't assume that quantity automatically produces quality. Don't settle for relating on the surface. Don't be satisfied with mysteries. Don't get lazy. Dig deep. Ask probing questions. Express your honest feelings. Confront. If your dating partner is by nature quiet, be gentle yet firm. Sensitively draw that person out. If he or she refuses to journey into deeper levels of communication, slow down. Reconsider the relationship or seek outside counsel. You will never find genuine intimacy with an uncommunicative partner.

CHEMISTRY!

And now the one you have been waiting for. The chemistry. The magic. The attraction factor.

The Bible tells a fascinating story about a man named Jacob who was smitten with love for a woman named Rachel. He was so attracted to her, in fact, that he wept with joy at the delight of finding her. Her father told Jacob he could marry her if he would first work for him for seven years. Jacob agreed, and Genesis 29:19 says that because of Jacob's great love for Rachel the seven years "seemed like only a few days." The wedding day came, and Jacob was dismayed to find that the dishonest father had given him Rachel's older sister. In order to have Rachel he had to commit to another seven years of work. As unbelievable as it sounds, he did it.

Jacob and Rachel were apparently drawn together by maximum magic. Such magic, however, is not unique to them. God designed all of us with the capacity to feel strongly attracted to potential partners. The Song of Songs beautifully acknowledges the progression of that attraction into the sexual intimacy of marriage. However, the kind of attraction the Bible extols is not just sexual attraction or passing infatuation.

While sexual attraction and infatuation focus almost exclusively on the physical aspects of face and form, a healthier, more mature attraction looks at the person as a whole. It says, "I marvel at this person's love for Christ. I respect her commitment to spiritual growth." It says, "I marvel at her strength of character. I respect her values and convictions, her courage, her honesty, her integrity." It says, "I marvel at the depth of communication we enjoy. I love the way we can open up our lives to each other and discuss root-level issues." And finally, "I marvel at the intensity of physical attraction I feel for her. I love the way God designed her frame and form. I love her body and her face and her hair. I can't believe how much I love her."

The trouble is, human beings have a remarkable tendency to jump into shallow attractions. They easily fixate on one aspect of another person and develop a heightened emotional response. *It can't be wrong if it feels so right* they say to themselves. But it *can* be wrong. Dead wrong.

That is why men and women who feel the intense pull of attraction *must* slow down and ask themselves some probing questions. Before they get their hearts wrapped up in relationships they can't get out of, they need to become painstakingly honest. Are we spiritually compatible? Do we truly respect one another's character? Do we both exhibit honesty, and responsibility, and vitality? Do we communicate openly? Have we really broken through the mystery and gotten to know one another well? If the answer to any of these questions is anything but a resounding *Yes!* then the attraction is not the healthy, whole-person attraction that leads to lasting romance.

Mature people learn to be wary of the fireworks that light up their lives from time to time. They know that not every little spark that glimmers holds the promise of lasting love. So, they don't jump to careless conclusions. They don't make fast moves. They don't avoid tough questions.

And they don't make regrettable mistakes.

Four

Time: The Acid Test

Las Vegas. The Kentucky Derby. The Illinois State Lottery. Publishers Clearinghouse Sweepstakes. Bingo.

Calculated risk—it's the name of the game. You lay something on the line, and you get something back . . . maybe. The key to winning is knowing how to figure the odds.

It is the same in the game of life, where every day presents choices involving calculated risks. Again, the people most adept at playing the game are those who have learned how to determine the safest bets.

It pays, then, to become a little bit street smart—to get around, to ask questions, to learn the score, to check the board in the infield before you bet on the horse. It pays to know when the odds are in your favor and when they are not.

THE HARD TRUTH

The oddsmakers say that at this time in Western culture the chances are five in ten that a marriage will lead to divorce. Flip a coin. Five out of every ten marriages will end up on the rocks.

They also say that if one or both partners are still teenagers, the odds for failing climb even higher. If either partner witnessed an unhappy marriage between mom and dad, the odds increase again. If one or both partners come from broken homes, the odds rise yet higher. If either partner has been divorced, the odds soar. If there has been regular sexual involvement before marriage, or if either or both partners abuse alcohol or drugs, the odds skyrocket.

The point is, the odds don't look good. In fact, they are frightening. And every sad statistic represents a couple who thought, *It will never happen to us*. But it did.

We live in an age of euphemisms; we don't like harsh language or straightforward analyses. So we talk about growing

73

apart, needing a change, breaking up, calling it quits, cutting our losses, starting over. But reality speaks louder than words. Divorce is not experienced euphemistically. The only words that do it justice are words like pain, soul-wrenching, broken hearts, destruction, grief, scars.

That is why we have, without apology, presented the wisdom of God. It is the only hope for reversing the odds. Why should we trust the vain speculations of a culture that doesn't have a clue about how to establish permanent relationships, when God has given us the blueprint for building marriages that *will last?*

A SAFE BET

So far in this book we have discussed the minimum requirements for a successful marriage: spiritual compatibility, character compatibility, communicational compatibility, and mutual attraction. No one should ever settle for a relationship that comes up short in any of those four areas.

But even these requirements leave a margin for error—a margin that can be reduced in only one way: the test of time. The old-fashioned sunup, sundown, day-after-day, week-after-week, month-after-month kind of time that reveals the truth. Short courtships require impulsive decisions about lifetime commitments. That is risky business, at best—and it's no way to beat the odds.

B Often when I greet people after services at our church, young couples announce their plans for marriage. After offering my congratulations, I always add a bit of free advice: "Go slow!" If that doesn't seem strong enough, I add some punch: "Go slower!!" If they ask me to officiate at their wedding I say, "Why don't you give me a year to think about it."

Go slow. *Go slow!* Few words of counsel can be so universally beneficial. Nothing tests the potential of a relationship like time. While there are scores of solid reasons for submitting to the test of time, in this chapter we want to address just three of them.

IS IT ... REAL?

Imagine you are reading this book in the elegant oak library of a statuesque colonial home. You are nestled comfortably in an overstuffed green leather chair flanked by two small, polished, octagonal tables. Twin lamps on the tables cast perfectly matched radials of light across the plane of your vision. You read for some time, then realize that you have unconsciously inched yourself toward the lamp on your left. The lamp on your right has dimmed to such a degree that you have become dependent upon the other one. You compare the lamps and find that while the one on your left is plugged into the main power source of the house, the lamp on the right is powered by a nine-volt battery—and it couldn't stand the test of time.

Infatuation and love both shine brightly at first, but infatuation proves to be hooked up to a nine-volt battery. As time passes, it fades. The intensity of the attraction diminishes. The romance cools off. The pulse rate adjusts to normal. Objectivity and good sense return. The formerly smitten young woman finds herself looking at the young man she was madly in love with just a month ago, and she thinks, *What was that all about? I fell head over heels for him?* The newly sensible young man looks at his almost-bride and thinks, *I was ready to march to the altar with her? I thought I could last a lifetime with someone like that?* Then they heave simultaneous sighs of relief and thank God that they subjected their attraction to the test of time.

Someone once defined love as "friendship that has caught fire." That is a far cry from the instant desire that characterizes infatuation. There is, of course, such a thing as immediate attraction. Undoubtedly, intense emotions can be unleashed at first sight, and sometimes these initial chemical reactions mature into real love. But not always; there is no guarantee. Only time can reveal the difference between infatuation and lasting love.

B Several months after we broke our engagement, I decided that the best way to get over losing Lynne was to start dating someone else. So I initiated a relationship with a very godly, blond Dutch girl who was an upstanding member of the Christian Reformed denomination to which

B I belonged. I didn't think she quite measured up to Lynne, but she certainly ran a close second.

I had been dating her for three or four months, and after one particularly enjoyable date, I began to think that maybe she was the one. It was a beautiful moonlit night; we were cruising down the highway in my spotlessly clean 1970 GTO; I still had Lynne's diamond ring in the glove compartment of my car (where she had left it when she exited), and I thought, *This girl would be just perfect. She's attractive. She's godly. She fits the ethnic/denominational preference of my family.* (Which Lynne didn't, by the way.) *I could give her this ring right now.*

The evening was right. The atmosphere was right. The emotions were right. I'm telling you, it was *right*. I was driving north on U.S. 131 toward Kalamazoo, with my hand on the gearshift knob, within eighteen inches of that glove compartment . . .

. . . *and within eighteen inches of the rest of my life!* I pondered the sudden proximity of the future, and I thought, *Everything seems right now, but what if this feeling goes away? What if she's not the one? What if I haven't given this thing enough time?* As it turned out, it did and she wasn't and I hadn't.

Four or five weeks later I thought, *She's all right, but she's not Lynne. She's not someone I want to commit my life to. What was I thinking?* She and I were compatible in a number of ways, and I was pleasantly attracted to her. But mere attraction isn't enough for marriage.

Attraction is an emotion that ebbs and flows. Only if attraction grows into genuine love does it become steady and stable enough to build a marriage on. And, generally speaking, four or five months isn't long enough to determine if an attraction will be sustained or temporary.

If an attraction is the real thing, if it is the kind of whole-person attraction that grows into lasting love, it will easily withstand the test of time. Jacob added seven years upon seven years and never lost his romantic desire for Rachel. During the testing time, one's pulse rate may moderate some, but if it is real love, the depth of feeling will not wane. The desire to be with the other person will increase. Appreciation for the other person will grow. One's sense of peace, tranquility, confidence, security, and joy in the relationship will deepen.

When young couples are unwilling to subject their attraction to the acid test of time, one must wonder what they are afraid of. What damage could it do to postpone the wedding for six months, a year, even longer? What are they afraid of? The truth? Are they afraid of what they might find out if they wait?

We have asked some couples those very questions. Sometimes the look in their eyes reveals that they are, in fact, afraid of the truth. We want to shake them and say, "Don't be foolish. Would you rather find out the truth after you're married? How do you think it would feel to live a lifetime with a faded infatuation?"

We dated for five years. During that time we broke up and got back together repeatedly, but the attraction never waned. In fact, it kept getting stronger and stronger. Each time we overcame an obstacle or resolved a conflict, we discovered more to respect about one another, more to talk about, more activities to enjoy together, more values we had in common, more goals that we shared, more complementary aspects of our personalities—in short, more reasons to love one another. The whole-person attraction that had drawn us together initially grew into a lasting love. It proved to be the Real Thing.

Not every couple needs to test their relationship for five years, but it sure makes for a safer bet than a five-*month* courtship. We suggest a minimum of one year of serious dating before a couple talks seriously of marriage. Eighteen months or two years is even better.

CONFIRM COMPATIBILITY

In addition to determining the nature of the chemical attraction between two people, time also affirms or erodes the other aspects of relational compatibility.

In an earlier chapter we discussed the importance of spiritual compatibility. It is crucial that spouses share a common treasure, look to a common blueprint for marriage, receive help from a common source of strength, and share common values. Because spiritual *in*compatibility always leads to frustration, conflict, and disappointment in marriage, young couples must *only* go with a sure bet in this regard. But how can they weigh the odds in their favor? How can they know for sure? Do they just take each other's word for it?

L I dated a guy one time with whom I desperately wanted to be spiritually compatible. He was kind, sensitive, responsible, and mature; I really liked him. But eventually I had to face the facts: Though he attended church with me and gave lip service to God, it was obvious that he didn't know Him in a personal way. I knew we could "talk Christianity," but I also knew we didn't truly share a common treasure. So I ended the relationship. I told him I did care for him, but I couldn't get seriously involved with someone who didn't share what was most important to me: a relationship with Jesus Christ.

That Sunday evening during church, the pastor invited people who wanted to publicly rededicate their lives to the Lord to come forward. Who was one of the first to get up out of his seat, walk all the way down the center aisle, and stand at the altar? The guy I had just broken up with. After the service, he tracked me down with the obvious intention of getting back together.

Was his commitment real? I hope it was. But I didn't have enough confidence in it to get involved with him again. It is easy to claim a spiritual commitment, and even to act convincingly spiritual for a period of time. Lots of people do it; there are numerous stories of men and women deceived all the way into marriage by partners who were living spiritual lies. But people can live the lie only so long—one month, three months, maybe six. But eventually they blow their cover. It is tough to fake spirituality for eighteen months, two years, three years. That is why the test of time is so important.

The parable of the sower in Matthew 13 tells us to be wary of seed that is sown on rocky soil. It springs up quickly because the soil is shallow. But when the sun comes up, the plants are scorched, and they wither because they have no roots. The plant looks good at first—just like a strong, healthy, deep-rooted one—but you have to watch it for a while to find out the truth. You have to wait and see what happens when the sun beats down upon it—when the pressure is on.

Have your partner's spiritual roots dug deep? Have they grown down into the hidden springs of Living Water? The only way to know is to apply the test of time. You have to watch, over a long period of time, a person's love for worship, for the Word, for prayer, for communion, for personal purity. You have to observe the consistency of his or her involvement in the body of Christ—in corporate gatherings, in small groups, in service.

When partners see each other's spirituality being tested and tried and found true, they can have confidence in their relationship. But if time reveals a waning spiritual drive or a fading devotion to spiritual concerns—if one person proves to be a spiritual sprinter rather than a long-distance runner—then the relationship should be terminated. As difficult and painful as that may be, it is far better to see the deception before the commitment is made.

The same is true in regard to character compatibility. Sadly, honesty, responsibility, and personal vitality can be counterfeited for longer than one would think. For months, dishonest people can cover their tracks and irresponsible people can use charm to appear responsible on the surface. And nearly anyone can give an impression of vitality and personal growth to someone who has known them only a short time. We have observed that determined people can counterfeit almost anything to get married. The only way to ferret out the counterfeit is time.

Waiting is a no-lose proposition. If character compatibility is proven over time, then the couple can move into marriage with confidence, security, and peace. If time flushes out deceitfulness or character weaknesses, then even in the midst of disappointment and hurt, there can be relief and thankfulness that the discovery was made before the knot was tied.

Even communicational compatibility must be tested by time. A couple must share a wide variety of life experiences to discuss and analyze together. They must experience enough true-to-life relational conflicts to see if they can communicate at a deep enough level to resolve them—not just minor ones, but major ones as well. They must acknowledge a broad range of feelings and become increasingly comfortable disclosing them. If over time they find that conversation is cooling down, and hostility is heating up—if more is being concealed and less revealed—then that is a neon warning sign. *Go slow! Go slower!*

MARS TO EARTH ... OVER

Our third reason for encouraging long courtships sounds, especially to young adults, like it comes from outer space. We know that. We have heard the groans and seen the eyes roll. But, truth is truth, no matter how strange it sounds.

So . . . here it is. Dating relationships must be submitted to the test of time so they can be affirmed by parents and Christian friends. You heard it here. *Affirmed by parents and Christian friends.*

The curse of our culture can be called by many names—the Lone Ranger Syndrome, the Marlboro Man Mentality, the My-Way-or-the-Highway Disease. Whatever you call it, this obsession with rugged individualism extends right into courtship. A couple embraces and defiantly shouts to onlookers: "We're adults now. We know we're right for each other. We don't need or want your approval. So stop butting into our lives!" With that attitude, they systematically cut themselves off from the input of those who may be the most caring and insightful people in their world—their parents and trusted friends. In most cases, who loves young men and women more than their parents? Who cheers for their happiness more than their closest friends?

The Bible challenges rugged individualists with words like these: "Submit yourselves, therefore, one to another." And: "In the abundance of counselors, there is much wisdom." To couples enjoying isolation in a bubble of love, these words are especially hard to hear. But often loving counsel can ward off outright disaster.

B   When we started getting serious and began talking about marriage, I sought my father's advice. I walked into his office, closed the door and said, "Dad, what do you think about Lynne? Do you think we're right for one another?"

B He looked me over, thought for a few seconds and said, "Marry her, Bill. You're no prize!" Knowing his sense of humor, I realized that he was affirming our relationship.

Unfortunately, Lynne's parents weren't so quick to approve. Several months after my conversation with my father, Lynne subjected our relationship to her parents. "What do you see in our relationship?" she asked them. "How should we proceed?" Their analysis? Trouble. *Big trouble*—spelled B I L L. And they were right. At that time I was not a very easy person to get along with. I was a serious Christian, but I still had a lot of rough edges— sharp edges like arrogance and insensitivity. They foresaw all kinds of problems in our relationship and didn't want Lynne to get hurt.

They suggested we break off the relationship for a year. They said, "If you go separate ways for a year and grow as individuals, then you can come back together and try again. If you can build a good relationship, we'll put our blessing on it."

You know the rest of the story. Lynne called off the wedding, and we didn't see each other for eighteen months. It was a very painful time for both of us.

But we can both say, without risking overstatement, that that time apart saved our relationship. Had we gotten married without the individual growth that year and a half provided we would have hurt each other so deeply that our marriage could not possibly have survived.

Several years ago a woman from our church called us and one of our church elders and submitted her future marriage to our scrutiny. Independently, we all counseled her not to go through with it. She was forty-five years old, deeply in love with the man, and well aware that she probably wouldn't have another chance at marriage. On top of that, the wedding was all planned. But she knew we were right, so she called it off. Since then she has thanked us profusely for saving her from a disastrous situation.

In a culture that flaunts its disdain of accountability, the idea of submitting to the scrutiny of others sounds unreasonable and unnecessary. But Christians need to learn that seeking godly counsel is wise. Opening a relationship up for analysis is part of determining the odds. Going slowly in courtship so others have time to observe and comment is part of calculating the risk.

We are not suggesting that counsel should be followed blindly. It should, however, be taken seriously, discussed thoroughly, and prayed about earnestly. The Bible teaches that the Holy Spirit speaks with one voice; He will not give different messages to different people. However, those who are caught up in the excitement of love and the anticipation of marriage often have a hard time deciphering the message, or they subconsciously refuse to hear it. So, the Holy Spirit often reveals insights through godly people who know and love the courting couple.

Sometimes parents cannot offer reliable insights because of emotional instability or personal immaturity. In such cases, the counsel of a parent substitute such as a church elder or small-group leader should be sought. Outside Christian counsel is also helpful when parents are not believers. It should be remembered, however, that even non-Christian parents can often provide invaluable insights if they know their children well and have their best interests at heart.

WHAT NOW?

But now let's say that time has proven the quality of the attraction and the compatibility. Let's say that all involved parties—the courting couple, parents, godly friends—sense the unmistakable seal of approval from the Holy Spirit. What now?

Let the wedding bells ring! Let there be celebration. Let the happy couple enter into a sacred covenant with God in the presence of affirming and encouraging parents and friends. Let there be laughter and joy and romance and honeymoons in exotic places. Let there be rejoicing in what God has done in bringing two of His children together.

But, if there is anything less than total agreement about the Spirit's leading, if either partner has any hesitation, if parents or trusted Christian friends can cite serious misgivings, if some areas of compatibility are developing unsatisfactorily—then *slow down*. For God's sake, for parents' and friends' sake, for future children's sake, for *your* sake, don't run to the altar. Slow the pace of the relationship. Break up for a while. Agree to wait another year. What is *one* year of waiting compared to forty years of pain? Don't say you can't. You can. Don't say it's too late. It's never too late.

L We were three months from our wedding when we called it off, and we didn't do it in a vacuum. Kalamazoo has a definite small-town atmosphere, and we were both very involved in the Christian community. A lot of people thought our breakup was big news. For us, it was more than a little embarrassing.

Facing the embarrassment, however, was the easy part. The hard part was losing one another. Even though I initiated the breakup, giving up Bill was absolute agony. Yes, we had our problems—serious ones—and I knew we had to part ways. But I certainly didn't want to. I had dated other guys—some wonderful, caring ones—but I had never felt for any of them a fraction of what I felt for Bill. My emotions had never been so tied to anyone before, and it was awful to break that tie. It was the hardest thing I have ever had to do. For days I cried. Whenever I heard his name I cried. Whenever I thought about him I cried. Months later, when I received an unexpected letter from him from South America, I cried.

But, I didn't regret my choice—even though I earnestly believed that our breakup was permanent. It was painful, but it was *right*. I knew that an unhappy marriage would be even more painful, and I preferred short-term pain to a lifetime of pain.

Again, the most miserable people in the world are not single people. They are married people who realize that their marriage was a mistake. Think how frustrating it must be to spend years trying to make an impossible situation work. Think how much energy it must take to keep a doomed relationship going.

Don't let that happen to you. Subject your relationship to the test of time. Find out whether your attraction is infatuation or lasting love. Test your partner's spirituality and character. See if your communication patterns continue to draw you closer together. Give parents and trusted friends time to observe your relationship, and then take their input seriously.

Please, don't make a risky play. Be patient. Be smart. Go slow so that when the time is right, you can enter marriage with confidence.

And you can beat the odds.

Part Two
Marriage That Lasts

Five

Exploring Family Backgrounds

Because both our dads were pilots, we both spent a good deal of time around planes and airports. We both took flying lessons in our teens (one of us got a license; the other got a date with the instructor). And we both learned that flying private planes is a dangerous sport.

To ensure higher levels of safety among private pilots, the FAA and officials of the private aircraft industry have collaborated to institute a host of rules and regulations. Top among them is the use of a series of safety checklists.

It starts with the preflight checklist. Pilots begin by examining the outside of the aircraft—the prop, wing surfaces, tires, oil, fuel caps, flaps, ailerons. Once inside the cockpit, they check the parking brake, charts and maps, radio frequencies, and other details. Finally they can hit the starter switch, but that doesn't mean they are ready to fly. First they have to go through the take-off checklist and inspect the gauges, power settings, navigational equipment, and trim tab. Then later there is a landing checklist for adjusted power settings, landing gear, flaps, and fuel tank selection. Student pilots almost need a checklist to check their checklists.

As tedious as these checklists can be, they prevent overenthusiastic pilots from jumping into planes, firing them up and taking off, and *then* finding out they are in serious trouble. It is a lot easier to solve a problem discovered on the ground than one discovered 5,000 feet above an ocean or a mountain range.

Obviously, the checklist system is too important to be ignored; still, many private pilots admit to cheating occasionally.

"I was so intent on getting airborne I just jumped in and took off."

"The day was too beautiful to waste on checklists."

"I was so excited I forgot all my careful training."

They all know they shouldn't do it. They are all aware of the possible consequences of carelessness. And they all end their confessions with good intentions for the future. Some of them, however, have to learn their lessons the hard way. . . .

B One sunny afternoon shortly after I got my pilot's license, I pulled my dad's high-winged plane up to the fuel pump and stayed in the cockpit while a young kid climbed a stepladder and filled the tanks. After I paid him and prepared to start the plane, I remembered that according to the checklist I should get out, climb the stepladder, and recheck the fuel caps. But I knew that the kid at the pumps was a responsible guy, so I just took off.

Bad choice. A short way into the flight I heard a loud banging noise over my head. While a bang in a car is no big thing—you just pull over and check it out—a bang in an airplane signals a major problem.

I tried to control my panic enough to figure out what the banging was. I checked the gauges, and there was the answer. The gas tanks I had just had filled were registering half empty. Obviously the kid at the gas pump had never put the gas caps on; the bang was caused by the caps dangling by their safety chains and pounding the top of the wing. Meanwhile, the fuel was quickly being sucked out of the tanks.

I can't describe how angry I was with myself. I kept thinking, *This is a terribly embarrassing reason for crashing.* A fighter pilot could radio in that he was going down because he took a missile from an enemy MIG. At least that would be a class reason for crashing; he'd go down in a blaze of glory. But there I was, sprinkling suburban lawns with airplane fuel, going down in a blaze of humiliation. I could hear it already: *Mayday, Mayday. I didn't check my fuel caps.*

Fortunately, I detected the problem soon enough (thanks to a not-so-subtle tip-off) to make a fast return to the airstrip before the fuel was gone. I escaped both humiliation and death, and I learned my lesson. Never

} again did I let the urge to be airborne overrule my better judgment. From that day on I have been devoted to checklists.

PREVENTING MARITAL MAYDAY

What about you? Have you learned the value of checklists? Have you submitted yourself to the premarital checklists contained in this book? Are you willing to search for potential problems while you are still on the ground?

The first four chapters of this book were our attempt to keep lovebirds from getting airborne prematurely and then discovering serious problems that may cause a crash. We talked first about the myths of marriage. How did you do on that checklist? Are you sure you are not expecting marriage to end your aloneness or heal your brokenness or ensure your happiness?

And then there was the compatibility checklist. Are you and your potential spouse spiritually compatible? Can you totally respect one another's character? Do you communicate on a deep level? Is your attraction based on an appreciation of the whole person?

And finally the time checklist. Have you dated long enough to be able to answer the previous questions confidently? Have parents and close friends affirmed your relationship?

If you have checked off all the items on those lists, you are probably in a serious dating relationship or even engaged. In the next few chapters we want to help you make your courtship count by drawing your attention to some tough issues that cripple many marriages. In this chapter, we want to look at differences in family background, an issue that is often ignored, but is fraught with more potential problems than most courting couples realize.

That was certainly true for us. Before we were married, we assumed we would face few conflicts in this area; we both grew up in healthy, happy, stable, Christian homes. Besides, we were marrying each other, not our families. What was there to worry about?

SO MUCH IN COMMON?

L When Bill and I started dating we thought it was quite extraordinary that both our fathers drove motorcycles,

L sailed boats, and flew airplanes. *They really have a lot in common,* we thought. That was very important to us because we both idolized our dads; we each thought every dad should be like ours. So we were pleased that these two wonderful men had such obvious points of contact.

What we did not realize was that in spite of their mutual interests these two equally wonderful men could not have been more different if they had tried. Even their approaches to cycling, sailing, and flying were opposite. Bill's father loved action and paid little attention to details such as maintaining his equipment. If his cycle sputtered enough to start, if his boat was tight enough to float, and if his plane lifted off the runway, he was happy. My father, however, enjoyed maintaining his equipment as much as— if not more than—using it. He spit-shined his cycle, customized his boat, and always kept his plane in peak condition.

They were just as different in their approaches to household maintenance. My father was the ultimate Mr. Fix-it. I don't recall Dad ever paying a repairman to come to our home. If something broke in our house, he fixed it. Refrigerator? Dryer? Furnace? Electrical system? Telephone line? Water softener? No problem. He had everything he needed; our garage was like a hardware store.

Bill's father took the exact opposite approach. He never fixed *anything* in the house. If a light bulb burned out he hired an electrician to change it. If a handle fell off a drawer he hired a carpenter to screw it back on. The only tool in the house or garage was a butter knife; when I went there for dinner I noticed that every butter knife had a twisted end.

As pronounced as the maintenance issue was, it was one of their less significant differences. More important were their differing approaches to family life. My father was extremely family centered. He preferred recreational activities that the entire family could engage in and never traveled without the family. In his late twenties he changed careers, leaving a job he loved to avoid evening work that cut into family hours.

L   Bill's father was very independent, with many interests outside the family. He traveled alone extensively, sometimes for pleasure, sometimes for business. It was not uncommon for him to be away from home for weeks at a time, a pattern which Bill easily learned to take in stride.

Our dads also differed in their basic fathering goals. My father grew up without the benefit of a strong, loving, involved father. He was determined to give his children what he hadn't received, and he succeeded. He was a very caring, sensitive, nurturing father, perhaps even to the point of being overprotective. I have no doubt that he spent many sleepless nights agonizing and praying over me. His primary means of expressing love were by offering time and emotional involvement, and by giving encouragement and affection. When he bought my first bike, he spent hours running along beside me, cheering me on and making sure I didn't take too many spills.

Bill's father grew up in a family of six sons, and though he was the youngest, he became the head of the family business. He was strong and rose to the challenge, and more than anything else he wanted to teach his children to rise to life's challenges. He rarely offered physical or verbal affection, but he lavishly expressed his love by providing opportunities that would stretch and challenge his children, that would help them become all they could be. When he bought Bill his first bike, he sent him down the street with a casual, "Hop on. You can do it." He knew a few tumbles would help prepare his son for the real world.

Bill's dad was a big-picture person; my dad enjoys the details. Bill's dad was an extravagant risk-taker; my dad calculates risk more cautiously. I could go on and on. . . .

But maybe you are wondering what the big deal is. So what if our fathers played with their toys and maintained their homes differently. So what if they approached work and travel and family time differently. So what if they had different ways of expressing love. They were both good men and good fathers. Why focus on the differences?

Here's why.

GREAT EXPECTATIONS

B It was the summer of 1974 and Lynne and I had been married two months. She informed me that the garbage disposal had quit working and I told her to call a repairman. The war was on.

"What do you mean, call a repairman? Why pay fifty dollars for a job any able-bodied man can do?"

"Well, you don't expect *me* to do it, do you? I don't know anything about garbage disposals. I'd probably electrocute myself if I touched it. Besides, we're short on butter knives."

"You could do it if you tried. You just don't care enough."

The problem was that Lynne's dad fixed things, her brother fixed things, her uncles fixed things, her cousins fixed things, and so she assumed that *all* men fixed things. Unless, of course, they weren't interested in what was going on at home. Unless they were too preoccupied with concerns outside the home to devote thirty minutes to household needs.

From my side, I had never had a success experience with anything mechanical in my life. I knew I would waste hours and probably money if I tried to fix the garbage disposal or anything else. I also believed, as my father had, that the sensible approach was to stick with what I was good at and pay someone else to do what I wasn't good at.

In retrospect we realize we were both out of line. Because Lynne's dad was so unusually capable in this area, Lynne had very unrealistic expectations of me. There was no way I could possibly have pleased her; I simply did not have the right skills. Also, she had always viewed her father's household help as an act of love, and wrongly interpreted my unwillingness to try to fix things as an indication that I didn't care about our home life. On the other hand, because my dad didn't repair anything around the house, I wouldn't repair anything either—even things I really could have fixed. And, because Lynne handled our finances, she knew that more often than not we couldn't afford a repairman. So, either the things wouldn't get fixed,

B or she would have to fix them herself. Actually, Lynne was pretty good at fixing things, but because of my workaholism, she was already handling more than her share of household responsibilities; she didn't want to have to be Mrs. Fix-it, too.

It took us a long time to get to the bottom of our extreme positions. We could have avoided a lot of conflict and frustration if we had talked through this issue before we got married. It would have helped me to know that Lynne's dad built televisions and houses and cars in his spare time. And it would have helped Lynne to know that my dad didn't know which end of the hose to hold to wash a car. Hopefully we would have adjusted our expectations accordingly.

While household repairs created a problem, they were nothing compared to the travel issue. Shortly before our first anniversary I announced that I was going on a vacation.

"Oh, great, where are we going?"

"No, you don't understand. I said *I* am going on vacation."

"Not without me you're not."

I couldn't believe her attitude. Why was she being so possessive and clingy and insecure and stubborn and selfish? What was her problem? Was she afraid to let me out of her sight? Did she think we had to do *everything* together? There was no way I was going to back down on this one. My dad used to call my mom from the airport and inform her that he was going to South Africa for five weeks. Why shouldn't I enjoy the same freedom?

But when I took off by myself (even for a few days) Lynne was convinced that I didn't love her. "Don't you like to be with me?" she asked. "Are you trying to get away from me?" Her father disliked spending even one night away from her mother. She couldn't understand why I sought the freedom of occasionally being on my own.

Eventually we settled into a pattern that we both enjoy—a pattern somewhere between the extremes of our parents. In fact, we've even flip-flopped some. Lynne frequently enjoys going off by herself, while I often find

B myself urging her to join me on trips. But we could have avoided a lot of hurt and misunderstanding in the early years if we had discovered this differing perspective while we were dating and had agreed on a compromise before the wedding.

We also had a big problem with expressions of affection.

Early in our marriage Lynne said to me, "Why don't we touch more and express our affection more freely?"

I said, "Why should we? I've lived without that for twenty-two years, and I don't need it now."

She said, "Well, I've lived with that for twenty-two years, and I do need it now."

We'd been aware of the affection difference during our courtship, but instead of talking about it, we made assumptions: I assumed she'd *grow out of it* once we were married, and she assumed I'd *get with it* once we were married. But neither of us changed, and the problem got worse. I thought she was overly sensitive, sentimental, insecure. She thought I was hard, distant, unloving.

How we wish we had looked more carefully at our backgrounds. Had Lynne realized that hugs and kisses and "I love you's" were not traded freely in my family she would not have interpreted my reserve as a lack of love. Had I realized how important they were in her family I would not have viewed her request as a sign of insecurity. And we probably could have met happily in the middle many years before we did.

Too often during our courtship we made assumptions about family issues we should have talked about. And during our marriage we paid.

CRITICAL QUESTIONS

We realize now that who our fathers and mothers were, how they related to one another, and how our families operated played a major role in shaping us as individuals. And that is true for everyone. Two decades spent in close proximity with a single group of people can't help but shape our personal identities. We are who we are largely because of the experiences we have enjoyed or endured within the context of our unique family units.

Family dynamics determine our self-esteem and self-confidence. Family values shape our character. Family experiences influence our concepts of how marriage should be structured and how children should be raised, and of how we should view work, recreation, education, money, politics, and religion. We all look at our families and decide either to repeat the pattern, if our experience was basically positive, or try to create an opposite situation, if our experience was basically negative. But either way, we are profoundly affected by the attitudes and actions of the family we grew up in.

Do you want to make your courtship count? Then talk in depth about your respective families. Describe your mom and dad. Talk about their personalities, their strengths and weaknesses, their talents and abilities, their hobbies, their jobs, their friendships. Talk about their marriage. Look at how they related to one another, expressed love, resolved conflicts, made decisions. Look at how they handled finances and divided household responsibilities and disciplined their children.

Describe the atmosphere of your home. Talk about how emotions were handled. Examine the values that held priority in your family and the behaviors that were rewarded. Describe the house you grew up in and discuss your family's standard of living. Talk about the forms of recreation your family enjoyed and your favorite family vacations. Share the experiences that shaped your self-esteem and built your self-confidence.

Tell how holidays and birthdays were celebrated. Discuss gift-giving practices. Tell what it was like to be sick when you were a child. Describe a typical mealtime conversation. Reveal secret bedtime routines. List the chores you were responsible for. Talk about how you related to grandparents, aunts and uncles, cousins.

In addition to promoting mutual understanding, such conversations can spark hopes and shape dreams for the future. Pleasant memories and treasured traditions can provide building blocks upon which a young couple can build their own marriage and family life.

THE INEVITABLE DOWNSIDE

Sadly, however, there are more to family memories than the highlights. In addition to being one of the greatest determiners of personal identity, the family is also one of the greatest causes of personal pain. No one grows up pain free. The apostle Paul tells us that no one can live a totally righteous life (Rom. 3:23), and that includes parents. There is no perfect mom. No perfect dad. We are all products of parents who were sinners. They too were products of parents who were sinners, just as our children will be. And imperfect parents always cause some degree of pain to their children. The baton that is passed from one generation to the next is always at least a little disfigured, a little scarred.

So, while it is important to talk about family highlights, it is even more crucial to discuss the lowlights. The problems. The painful memories. The disappointments. The things you hope will never be repeated in your own home.

A discussion of lowlights may be one of the most difficult and unnatural conversations a couple can have. Most of us have an overwhelming urge to defend the families we grew up in. We feel disloyal when we reveal negative family dynamics to outsiders. It helps to remember that every family—even the best of them—has a shadow side. And every young man and woman has some degree of pain, some little disappointment, some slight scar that remains long after he or she has left the family home. Those things must be discussed because they always—*always*—produce some kind of backlash. And the deeper the problem, the fiercer the backlash.

A friend of ours grew up in an extremely hostile home. His father was a tyrant who ordered his kids around and slapped them into submission. On the surface the kids cowered in fear; underneath, they seethed with anger. They were never allowed to verbalize either the fear or the anger. Five years into marriage, our friend's wife was shocked by a sudden change in her husband. He became distant, stubborn, rebellious. They went to a counselor and discovered that the fear and anger that had poisoned his youth were making their inevitable claim on his adult life. Together they worked through it, but it wasn't easy.

A woman we know was frustrated by her lack of sexual desire for her husband. She loved and respected him, found him physically attractive, and desperately wanted to experience true sexual oneness with him. But she could never offer more than a physical response; her inner feelings never matched her actions. Finally she went to a counselor and uncovered a story of sexual abuse. She had never been raped, but repeated episodes of inappropriate touching by a family member had left their mark. To avoid the emotional pain of the abuse she had learned to shut down her sexual feelings; years later, in each intimate encounter with her husband, her feelings shut down automatically. Awakening them took her on a long and painful journey.

Another woman we know was a sincere and growing Christian, but she never felt like she measured up to God's expectations. She never felt like she was serving enough, or praying enough, or giving enough, or growing enough. So she pushed herself until she became chronically overscheduled, stressed-out, negative, and unhappy. She came to our church counseling center when she realized that her frame of mind was destroying her relationship with her husband. Her problem was one that afflicts many devout Christians. She had grown up in a rigid, legalistic environment and viewed God as a commanding officer issuing long lists of harsh orders and withholding praise from all but the most intense. Hers was a God one could fear, but hardly love. Our counselor convinced her that the demanding God of her parents was not the giving God of Scripture. Eventually she dropped her burdens, learned to love God freely from a joyous heart, and began to serve in healthy, constructive ways. Her husband rejoiced in the changes her new outlook produced in their marriage.

What is the common point of these diverse examples? That the shadow sides of our family experiences—whether they involve false values, mistaken beliefs, harsh behaviors, abuses, misunderstandings, or disappointments—profoundly affect us as adults and marriage partners. It is imperative, therefore, that we share with one another the downside, that we ask and answer the tough questions. What are your most painful childhood memories? What was your biggest disappointment? Did you ever feel unloved or neglected? Was there emotional or physical or sexual abuse in your home? Were either of your parents alcoholics? Were your parents divorced?

The obvious benefit of answering these questions is that it helps partners understand one another better. Another benefit is that sometimes it helps partners understand *themselves* better. Openly discussing our past with someone with whom we feel safe and comfortable often helps us discover things about ourselves—sometimes unpleasant or unhealthy things—that we hadn't been aware of before. Once the problems come out into the open, they can be dealt with so they won't come back to haunt the marriage later on.

Recently we had dinner with an engaged couple. The young man spoke openly about the pain of being raised by a father who never gave his full approval to anything his son did. "With my father," he said, "nothing was ever enough. An A minus should have been an A. Two touchdowns should have been three. Vice president of the class didn't make it; I should have been president." His eyes started to water as he grabbed his fiancée's hand. They had spent hours and hours discussing this wound. They had gone to counseling so she could better understand how that dynamic had affected him and how it would affect their relationship, and so he could learn constructive ways of dealing with the pain. We were so impressed with their mature perspective. They were using their courtship to build the foundation for an emotionally healthy future.

We know another young man and woman who are both children of alcoholics. Because they were keenly aware of the scars they bore, they each began seeing a counselor and attending Al-Anon meetings long before they even considered engagement. By the time they married, they each had an arsenal of insight and strength and maturity. In spite of their troubled pasts, they went on to build a solid, happy, God-honoring marriage.

What was the key to their success? They faced their potential problems and did something about them—before they got married. They determined not to carry weakness, pain, and misunderstanding down the aisle. They refused to let painful pasts poison their future.

Talking about the past can be a rich, trust-building experience as partners learn that it is okay to be real, that there are no wounds, no secrets, no memories too embarrassing to reveal. And it can foster the oneness God had in mind for marriage as partners share an ownership of each other's past and a mutual respect for each other's journey.

NOW IS THE TIME

Too often courtship is devoted to fancy dates and superficial conversations. Don't make that mistake. Make your courtship count by plunging beneath the surface. Find out who your partner really is by digging into the past, by looking closely at the family he or she grew up in.

Couples often think they will have more time to talk about family background after they are married, but that seldom happens. Adult responsibilities usually eat up more time than young couples anticipate. Unrushed dinners in quiet restaurants often become things of the past. By necessity, conversations focus on career and household and child-rearing responsibilities. The time to talk about the past is now, during courtship.

In addition to talking about family background, you should make it a point to spend time with one another's family so you can make your own observations and come to your own conclusions. If you are uncomfortable with your partner's family, you should spend even more time with them. Try to discover why you feel that way, then discuss your concerns with your partner. Don't make accusations or have a critical spirit, but be honest and open. You must face the facts. If your partner hopes to emulate his or her family, and you aren't comfortable with how that family operates, you have a serious problem. You shouldn't ignore it.

If thorough discussions uncover major differences, please postpone your wedding and seek help from a trained counselor. If further probing reveals uncompromisable differences and expectations, you must be courageous enough to part ways. Moving into marriage with built-in conflicts is a sure route to heartache and pain.

Six

Resolving Temperament Tensions

It was charming, quaint, cozy—a limestone cottage flanked by giant evergreens. Sunlight sneaked between the graceful branches, filtered through the sheer curtains, and bounced off the golden walls of the peaceful sitting room. A woman read quietly in an easy chair, a brown-eyed spaniel at her feet, while her husband busied himself with pleasant domestic chores. The young couple, newlyweds, had created in their humble abode a refuge from life's storms and had welcomed into their hearts and home two young men with no other home to claim; the four lived together in joy and harmony. When the afternoon sun began to fade the woman moved cheerily to her small but well-provisioned kitchen and prepared a feast to delight her grateful companions. Round the bountifully laden table they gathered, and the young husband offered a simple but heartfelt prayer. There hovered an aura of love.

That's the way it was, all right—in our dreams. In reality, the years we spent in our first home were anything but the fairy tale just described. The only thing quaint about our tan brick house was its size: It was downright minuscule. The lot upon which it perched was so narrow we didn't even have room for a driveway. And the evergreens didn't flank it; they overran it. There was no way the sunlight could have sneaked between the tangle of unkempt greenery that shrouded our uncurtained windows. The golden glow that filled the living room was nothing more than the gaudy glimmer of our high-gloss canary yellow walls. The woman of the house never had time to read, and her husband avoided domestic chores at all costs. The brown-eyed spaniel? Yes, he was there, as were a black-eyed littermate and two other large dogs. The two springer spaniels were ours; the German shepherd and the Doberman belonged

101

to our two long-term boarders. These young men may have been looking for a refuge from life's storms, but they sure didn't find it in our home. The walls of our tiny cracker box groaned against the cumulative force of four busy adults and four active dogs. Chaos, not joyful harmony, reigned. Nor did we enjoy many sumptuous meals. There was not a decent cook among us, and even when we combined our meager earnings we could barely afford the simplest food. And the loving atmosphere? It left the house shortly after we moved in.

It was in that house, in fact, that we first began to suspect that perhaps our marriage had been a mistake. An observer might have blamed our marital frustrations on external circumstances: too many people in too small a space, or too little money, or too busy a schedule. And perhaps these factors did exacerbate our conflicts. But we both knew there was a deeper problem, something far more fundamental. We feared that on our wedding day we had made the most devastating mistake of our lives.

L   I clearly remember standing in our tiny living room at 2001 South Ashland, staring out the window at the evergreens, tears streaming down my cheeks.

"I can't believe I did this. How could I have been so stupid?"

I was angry, frustrated, fearful. It was like a terrible dream, but I couldn't wake myself up. I felt trapped and hopeless and confused. It suddenly seemed so obvious: I had married the wrong person.

What happened? I kept asking myself. *How did I get here? Where did I go wrong? And what do I do now?*

I shuddered under the shocking realization that the one I had pursued so earnestly, the man of my dreams, the person I had once feared I could never have, was now someone I wished I had never met. It was post-honeymoon blues at their worst. It was the ultimate buyer's remorse.

It was a terrible feeling, and sadly, one that is familiar to many. Almost every person who walks a wedding aisle comes to a point in the development of the marriage relationship when he or she says, "I think I made a terrible mistake. I think I married the wrong person."

Often people in the throes of fear and confusion say things like this: I don't feel like I know my spouse anymore. We had so much in common while we were dating, but now we seem to see everything differently. This isn't the person I fell in love with. My spouse has changed so much.

Actually, the spouse has probably changed very little. But reality often reveals what romance conceals. In the day-to-day routine of real life spouses begin to notice things they hadn't seen before. They tend to focus on their differences rather than the common beliefs or interests that drew them together, they tend to become irritated by the idiosyncrasies that charmed them when they were dating, and they tend to look at the negative side of the very qualities they most admired in one another before they were married.

That is what happened to us. During our courtship, our feelings flourished in the rich soil of our obvious compatibility. We held in common our deepest values and our highest goals. We respected one another. We enjoyed an intense whole-person attraction for one another. Our problem was that we focused all our attention on these delightful points of contact and neglected to pay attention to some important points of difference. We didn't look at the differences in our family backgrounds discussed in the previous chapter, or the differences in our basic personalities.

Our failure to pay careful attention to our personality differences was a mistake for which we have paid a high price. We are convinced that the history of our marriage could have been written in far more pleasant terms if we had stumbled upon the ideas presented in this chapter during our courtship rather than fourteen years into our marriage.

Some of the ideas presented in the next few pages were previously discussed in *Honest to God?* (a book by Bill Hybels), in a chapter called "Mutually Satisfying Marriage." We think they are so important, however, that we decided to present them in an updated form in this chapter.

THE SPICE OF LIFE

Experts in the field of personality development teach that just as human beings are born with blue eyes or brown eyes, with black hair or blond hair, tall or short, so they are born with predispositions toward certain ways of thinking, behaving, and viewing the world. In the 1950s Isabel Myers and Katharine Briggs expanded on Carl Jung's work on differing temperament traits and devised a test for identifying personality types based on varying combinations of these inborn traits. This test became known as the Myers-Briggs Type Indicator.

One book that takes an in-depth look at Jung's theory and the applications made by Myers and Briggs is *Please Understand Me* by David Keirsey and Marilyn Bates.[1] It has been of great help to us. By focusing on four aspects of thought and behavior, this book has helped us see some of the different ways in which people approach thinking and behaving. These diverse ways of thinking or behaving are called preferences. Each preference spans a continuum from mild to moderate to extreme. If you find it easy to "see yourself" in a given description on the following pages, you probably have an extreme preference in that area. If the picture isn't quite as clear, you may have only a mild preference.

The first potential difference deals with sources of emotional energy and how they affect people's relational patterns. Some people are *introverts* who derive energy from solitude. They enjoy spending lots of time alone and usually tend toward pursuits that afford quiet isolation. An extreme introvert might choose to go jogging alone rather than join an exercise class, and would be more likely to read a self-help book than attend a personal growth seminar. If you ever see anyone playing eighteen holes of golf alone, you can bet he or she is an introvert.

Introverts think before they speak and usually say little. They prefer a few close friends rather than many acquaintances, and would often opt for a quiet night at home rather than a social get-together. They may be warm, caring, and friendly toward people, but social interaction drains them—they feel slightly uncomfortable in groups—so they need a heavy balance of energizing solitude. They need to get alone where they can relax, "let down," and be themselves again.

Extroverts, on the other hand, derive energy from interaction with people. Most extroverts enjoy working and playing on a team. They usually have many friends and spend much of their time with others. Extreme extroverts love nothing more than a party, and usually end up being the life of it. They tend to talk a lot; in fact, it sometimes seems they have to talk in order to figure out what they think. Extroverts enjoy solitude now and then, but too much of it drains them emotionally. They need the inspiration of interaction to keep their batteries charged.

One time after a flight, we were shuttled to our hotel by a middle-aged extrovert who generated a nonstop conversation for an hour and a half. When we asked him how he liked his job, he said, "I love it. I spend twelve hours a day, six days a week, driving people back and forth from the airport. We have a great time, talking, joking, laughing, sharing stories. What could be better than that? I hate to go home at night."

While introverts and extroverts differ in their approach to social interaction, sensers and intuitives differ in their approach to gathering and utilizing information. If *sensers* were to describe themselves in one word, it would probably be "practical." Sensing people "want facts, trust facts, and remember facts."[2] They have their feet firmly planted in reality. Giving little thought to what might have been or what may be in the future, they focus on what really happened or what is. They look to the past, learn through experience, and highly value other people's experiences. When "sensing" employers interview potential employees, they tend to focus questions on the applicants' history, reasoning that past experience is the best basis for assuming future productivity.

Sensers are unusually accurate in observing detail because they prefer to take in information through their senses: what they see, hear, smell, feel, and touch. After parties sensers can often describe in accurate detail what all the guests wore, exactly how the room was decorated, and what songs played in the background. If asked to describe the event, extreme sensers would likely provide more details than many of their listeners would care to know.

Intuitives would probably describe themselves as "innovative." For them, what *is* can always be improved upon. Their vague sense of dissatisfaction with reality propels them toward change. The future intrigues them far more than the past or present, and they are fascinated with ideas and possibilities. Intuitive employers interviewing prospective employees tend to pay more attention to what the applicant says regarding the future of the organization than what he or she has done in the past.

Intuitives delight others with their speculation, imagination, creativity, and poetic imagery, but because their heads are often in the clouds, they are subject to error regarding facts and details. After parties, intuitives may well remember only those details related to their current preoccupation.[3] If asked to describe the evening, extreme intuitives would likely sum it up in a metaphor, and leave their sensing listeners feeling "in the dark" and longing for more concrete information.

While sensers solve problems through careful analysis of the facts, intuitives often find complex solutions coming to them "out of nowhere." These frequent hunches lead intuitives down a variety of paths; in fact, they tend to skip from one activity to the next, often relying on others to finish what they started. They are often "big-picture" people who need someone else— usually a senser—to fill in the details. Sensers often see intuitives as flighty, impractical, and unrealistic, while intuitives accuse sensers of being mired in minutiae and slow to see possibilities.

A third category—that of thinkers and feelers—shows how people differ in the area of assessing choices and making decisions. *Thinkers* take a logical approach to life, preferring to let their heads rule. They tend to be cool and calculated, cut and dried. They concern themselves with right and wrong, with prudence, with goals, with efficiency. In the legal system, they cry for justice. In business, for productivity and profit. In education, for unwavering truth. If something is right, they do it. If something is fair, they promote it. If something makes sense, they pursue it.

A manager who is a thinker says, with little trauma or emotion, "I'm sorry, Joe. We've adjusted your job description three times, and you're still not making the grade. It will be better for the company and for you if you look for something else." A teacher who is a thinker says, "You should have stayed after school if you didn't understand the assignment. I can't change your grade now. That would be unfair to the kids who did the assignment properly." A parent who is a thinker says, "Don't argue with me, Tony. You knew the rules and you broke them. Now you have to pay the consequences. I hope you learn your lesson."

Feelers prefer to let their hearts rule. They feel deeply themselves and empathize easily with how others feel. They tend to base their decisions on how their choices will affect others. They hate it when people feel sad or hurt or discouraged, and long to be able to ease their pain. They prefer mercy over justice, put people ahead of profits, and sometimes see gray where thinkers see black and white.

Feelers in management agonize over difficult personnel decisions. "Yes, you're right. Joe probably will be better off in another job. But he has tried so hard, and I hate to make him feel like a failure." Feelers in education lose sleep over children who don't make the grade. "I know Angela really doesn't deserve a better grade. But I hate to penalize her for misunderstanding the assignment." Feelers who are parents really mean it when they say to their kids, "This hurts me more than it hurts you."

Thinking and feeling preferences have nothing to do with levels of intelligence or the ability to analyze and get to the root of complex issues. The question is: Once I see the issue, is it more natural for me to decide according to my head or according my heart?

People also differ in how they structure their lives. Some people are highly organized and love lists and rules and schedules. They like to maintain a fairly predictable routine and can become irritated by interruptions. They like to know the plan and stick with the program. Their motto is: *Just settle it*. They don't like surprises, and change can cause them anxiety. They tend to be serious and perfectionistic, and sometimes pessimistic. They are extremely conscientious, take responsibilities seriously, meet deadlines with time to spare, and seldom feel free to play until their work is done.

Other people feel trapped when life is organized, and prefer freedom and spontaneity. Their natural tendency is to play before they work, and some of them take their work seriously only when staring a deadline in the face. They hate to live by schedules and hesitate to finalize plans. Their motto is: *Play it by ear*. They like to keep as many options open for as long as possible. They thrive on change and unpredictability. They tend to be lighthearted, playful, and optimistic. They view every day as an adventure and can't wait to see what comes along.

B My dad was the ultimate "play it by ear" guy. One time when I had accompanied him to Washington, D.C. for business, he concluded his work with a few days to spare, so he suggested that we travel somewhere else.

"Where did you have in mind?" I asked.

"Well, Billy, what do you say we just walk into National Airport and get on the first plane to *anywhere?*"

That's exactly what we did! We missed the plane to London by about thirty seconds, but ended up in Jamaica, not a bad second choice.

The next two areas of difference, the initiator/responder[4] difference and the task/relationship difference, are not part of the Myers-Briggs Type Indicator, but we have found them to be helpful supplements. Bob Phillips explains them in his book, *The Delicate Art of Dancing with Porcupines*.[5]

Initiators create ideas and action. They are aggressive, assertive, and willing to confront. They tend to be outspoken, often talking loudly and quickly, and adding emphasis with intonation and body language. Initiators make decisions easily, and express them with directness and intensity. They know how to take charge and like to do it. They can be excellent leaders, though they sometimes seem overwhelming to others.

Responders prefer to let other people's ideas and actions come their way. They are less assertive and aggressive than initiators, and avoid confrontations whenever possible. They are indecisive and cautious, and tend to speak quietly and unemotionally, hesitating to express their opinions for fear of imposing on others. They listen carefully, avoid the use of power if at all possible, and have a generally supportive attitude. Others view them as shy, but likeable.

The difference between initiators and responders is evident in a variety of situations. We have observed on our son's sports teams that children who are initiators tend to excel at offense, while responders often excel at defense. Young responders frequently seem to feel more comfortable defending their nets against oncoming soccer balls than trying to create action on the front line. Meanwhile, initiators seem to prefer the challenge of scoring goals.

People also differ in being either task oriented or relationship oriented. *Task-oriented* people tend to prioritize tasks above relationships. They feel best when they are accomplishing something tangible. If they are planning a dinner party, the details of the evening—food, decorations, seating arrangements, parking, entertainment—will be their primary concern. They will prefer to spend the evening attending to their organized list of nonrelational tasks.

Relationship-oriented people, on the other hand, place relationships ahead of tasks. When they plan a party, they hope someone else will handle the details, so they can greet the guests, make them feel at home, and spend the evening mingling.

WHY AREN'T YOU NORMAL LIKE ME?

This list is far from exhaustive. There is an almost infinite number of ways in which people can and do differ. And that is great. The intermingling of diverse personalities, unique outlooks, and complementary strengths is often the key to success in the marketplace, in education, in the church, in family life, and even in marriage.

The old adage about opposites attracting tends to be true, and for good reason. Opposites challenge one another, enhance one another, and, especially during courtship, fascinate one another. But the fascination often leads to frustration. Though we are drawn to people who are different from us, we have a hard time figuring them out. Eventually the mystery leads to misunderstanding, and too often the misunderstanding leads to maligning.

It can get downright ugly.

A previously adoring couple ends up trading blatant putdowns: *You don't make sense. You are strange. There is something wrong with you. Why aren't you normal like me?* The ultimate odd couple, they come to the only conclusion that seems to make sense: that they married the wrong person.

But did they? Would they really be better off if they had married someone just like them?

A PERSONAL CASE STUDY

B   I married Lynne because I respected her character and her spiritual commitment, I enjoyed the way we related as equals, and I was attracted to her physically. In addition, I was challenged and stimulated by our obvious differences. In nine out of ten areas of possible difference, we seemed to be at opposite ends of the continuum.

For example, Lynne was much quieter than I was and had fewer friends. She was warm and friendly toward people, but in groups she was reserved and preferred a few close friends rather than many casual acquaintances. She didn't talk a lot, but what she said was always worth listening to. I didn't know about introverts and extroverts back then. All I knew was that I was intrigued by the aura of substance, depth, and mystery that surrounded her.

She was also much more tender, caring, sensitive, and kind than I was. I knew I was off the charts as an unemotional, calculating thinker, and I thought I should probably have a heart someday. *Maybe it will help to marry one,* I thought. *Maybe we can just share hers.*

Lynne was also more structured and organized than I. For myself I preferred a more spontaneous approach to life, a make-it-up-as-you-go kind of approach, but I found her penchant for planning rather charming. Her life was very much in order; she was highly responsible; she knew how to cover the bases and handle the details and keep things running smoothly. It was fascinating to watch her in operation.

But several years into our marriage the fascination turned to frustration. I began to resent some of the very qualities that had attracted me to her initially.

To begin with, I decided she was *too* quiet. She was almost uncommunicative, it seemed to me. I had to draw everything out of her, and it was too much work. I wanted someone I could have easy conversations with. I wanted someone who didn't weigh every thought and word so carefully.

And she didn't have near enough friends. I kept trying to push her into relationships, but she wouldn't cooperate.

B   "I didn't know I was signing up to do duty with a
hermit," I shouted.

"Go away and leave me alone," she whispered.

"That's the problem. You always want to be left alone.
You always want *us* to be left alone. I want a social life. I
want parties and picnics. I want Super Bowl bashes with so
many people crammed together in the same room that they
sweat!"

"You are sick! You superficial extroverts are all alike—a
mile wide and an inch deep. You think the answer to
everything is a party. Go ahead and invite the whole world
over if you want to. Just don't invite *me*."

She had a real problem in the relational/social area, but
that wasn't her only one. She was also way too tender.
Sensitivity and compassion are fine—in moderation. But
she would sniffle through movies and sob if a friend's dog
died.

And then there was the structure issue. She simply could
not live with question marks. She always wanted to know
the plan—like where we were going on vacation, when we
were leaving, and when we were coming home—in
advance!

That was just the beginning of my list of resentments.
Our differences went on and on. I expressed some of my
frustrations to Lynne in my world-renowned sensitive and
constructive way. Others I kept inside where they could
smolder and create hostility. Both methods of dealing with
them caused more harm than good, fueled our already
inflamed emotions, and broadened the distance between
us.

But then God began chipping away at my self-centered-
ness, my narrow-mindedness, and my immaturity. As He
did that I began to see Lynne again through the eyes with
which I had first seen her. And now I've come back full
circle to a deep appreciation of the differences between us.

Because Lynne is an introvert our home is a safe and
tranquil place. It is a refuge. My life is crowded to
overflowing with people—neighbors, friends, colleagues,
staff, church members—and involvements that stretch and
drain me. If I came home to a flaming extrovert who

B wanted to throw a block party every three days I would go nuts.

Because Lynne enjoys time alone and loves to learn, she reads a lot. Then, what she reads she brings to our relationship. Not long ago on our Thursday morning breakfast date she told me about a book she was reading about what it was like to grow up in Europe during World War II. There I sat in that restaurant, getting a mini-course in history for the price of a bowl of oatmeal.

I see now that Lynne's ability to *feel* so deeply is what moves her to care for people in ways that are not natural for me. She is the one in our house who writes out the checks to third-world ministries. She is the one who organizes blanket drives for people living in cardboard boxes. She is the one who dug ditches at an orphanage in Mexico. She is the one who pulls me aside after church services and tells me how my flippant remarks can pierce someone's soul. She is the one who has taught me how to treat our son, Todd, whose tender heart could have been crushed by my insensitivity.

I also need a wife who knows how to keep life in order. Thanks to Lynne's preference for structure, we have an organized home. We have clean clothes. We have a healthy diet. We have a budget that works. We have two children who know how to sit down and finish their homework. And I have to admit that some of our adventures have actually been enhanced by her thoughtful planning.

Many times I was tempted to take out a hammer and chisel and reshape Lynne into a replica of me. I even tried a little now and then. Thank God I didn't succeed. I realize now that one of me is plenty in our home. I bet one of you is plenty in your home too.

A BETTER WAY

The hammer and chisel routine was a chore we shared. We each believed that we were the standard for what was right, normal, acceptable, even godly. And we each did our valiant best to get the other "shaped up." Then one year on vacation we read together that wonderful book on temperament we've previously cited called *Please Understand Me*. The title echoed our hearts' cries, and the content both chastised and encouraged us. We were chastised for our mutual arrogance in trying to force our preferences on each other. We were encouraged by the realization that we could both be right, normal, acceptable, and godly—even if we were opposite. We could be different without being wrong or right.

Reading that book marked a turning point in our relationship. We quit trying to minimize our differences, and decided to celebrate them instead. We decided to give each other the freedom to be who God made us to be.

L Previously I had felt threatened by Bill's desire to spend so much time with other people. I thought that meant he wasn't happy with me. When I learned that extroverts *need* the stimulation of a variety of relationships, I could sincerely encourage him to enjoy his many friendships.

We also consciously focused on ways that our different perspectives and preferences complemented each other.

L In the past I had judged Bill as cruel and heartless because he didn't empathize with others as easily as I did. I learned, however, that I could benefit from his more objective perspective. Sometimes I felt too sorry for people and "rescued" them when I should have let them face the consequences of their mistakes. Bill helped me look beyond the immediate need to the future implications and the lessons people needed to learn. Conversely, Bill discovered that sometimes he needed to let my perspective soften his; he needed to let justice give way to mercy.

I have also learned from Bill to loosen up a little in regard to structure. I still generally prefer to plan ahead and maintain an orderly routine, but I've discovered that splashing the routine with a little spontaneity now and then can add fun to life and enhance relationships. This is particularly true in parenting. Some of the best times I have shared with my kids were spur-of-the-moment events I probably would have missed had I not been influenced by Bill's make-it-up-as-you-go approach to life. Of course,

L there have been other wonderful parenting moments we both would have missed had I not carefully planned them.

Bill and I have found our initiator/responder differences to be especially complementary. Bill is the consummate initiator. He generates ideas and action without even trying, proposing far more options than he could ever develop on his own. I have energy and enthusiasm, but I often don't know where to channel them. We have discovered that we can be extremely productive as a couple when I throw my energy behind his ideas. This book is a prime example. So many times during the writing process, Bill tossed an idea into the air, and I caught it, developed it, and put it on paper. I could have thought for days and not come up with an idea as good as his. He could have played with his idea for days and never have developed it.

Discovering the complementary nature of previously frustrating differences is one of the surest indicators of a healthy marriage.

Not all differences are complementary, however. Sometimes instead of struggling to mesh our differences, we need to openly admit that they don't mesh and find creative ways to work around them. We discovered this in the realm of our Christian service.

L   During the early years of our marriage we led couples' discipleship groups in our home. Bill loved it, but I always felt burdened by the responsibility of maintaining close, accountable relationships with five or six women each week. When we learned about the difference between introverts and extroverts we realized why I didn't enjoy, or feel effective, leading groups. After that, Bill began leading men's groups, and I focused on an area of service more in line with who God made me to be—writing articles on spiritual growth for the journal published by our women's ministry. The printed page proved to be a far more effective way for me to "disciple" women than meeting in small groups.

Recently Bill mentioned this in a sermon. Afterward, a young couple approached him with tears in their eyes. "I

L needed to hear this," the husband said. "I have been giving my wife a hard time for not joining me in an evangelistic marketplace ministry. She is always wanting to get involved with ministries to the poor, but I thought we should be serving together. Now I realize I was wrong. It's okay for me to do marketplace ministry, and her to serve the poor."

A few weeks later I received a letter from the wife. She told me that her husband had just led several businessmen to the Lord, and that she had just joined a volunteer league that serves the inner-city homeless. "We're both happy," she said, "and we each know that we are making a difference."

It is still a challenge for us to give one another freedom to be ourselves. Sometimes we are nearly overwhelmed with the temptation to wield the chisel again. But then we remind ourselves that being opposite doesn't mean one of us is wrong. It just means we have to work a little harder to celebrate each other's uniqueness.

YOUR ONE AND ONLY?

Why is it so important to understand that? Because sometimes when couples discover how different they really are, they jump to the conclusion that their marriage is hopeless, that they might as well give up because they chose the wrong spouse. Sometimes well-meaning Christians contribute to their sense of hopelessness.

We once heard a pastor say, "Somewhere on planet earth there is a special someone just for you. God designed this person before the foundations of the world to be your lifetime mate." This is the "one and only" theory, and suggests that out of the five billion human beings that inhabit planet earth, God prepared one—and only one—to be your spouse.

This theory appears harmless, but it can be downright dangerous for a couple who is trying hard to make their marriage work, but making little headway. They are frustrated, but they keep plodding along until they stumble upon the "one and only" theory. Suddenly a light bulb goes on. *Here's our problem. You're not my one and only, and I'm not yours. This marriage will never work. We missed. God can't bless this marriage, so why keep hitting our heads against brick walls? Let's part ways and find our one and only.* Their assumption is that if they find their one and onlys, marriage will be easy. They won't have to make compromises, or work through conflicts, or negotiate family differences, or wrestle with temperament issues. It will be smooth sailing on the seas of wedded bliss . . . if only they find their one and onlys. Even those whose convictions will not let them part ways live with the burden of regret. *I missed my one and only.*

While this notion has been bantered around in Christian circles for years, we find little biblical support for believing that God ordained every marital match before the foundation of the world. As in many other areas of Christian living, the Bible lays out broad parameters for spouse selection. Within those parameters, individuals have the freedom to choose. In 1 Cor. 7:39 Paul says that a woman whose husband dies "is free to marry anyone she wishes, but he must belong to the Lord." Certainly Paul would tell her—and us—to choose carefully: to go through the proper checklists, move slowly, pray for guidance and sober judgment, and seek wise counsel. But then we are free to use our brains, examine our hearts, and select the spouse we feel best suits us. If we choose wisely, under His guidance, God promises the grace, courage, wisdom, and power needed to build our marriages.

If some years later we second-guess the wisdom of our choice, God says, "Don't look backward. The decision has been made. Look forward. Face the challenges head on. I'll walk with you as you build this marriage. If it gets rough, seek help from friends. If you get stuck, see a counselor. But don't waste time wondering if you missed your one and only. As far as I am concerned, *you are married to your one and only.* So get on with the task of making your marriage flourish. Turn to Me with humble hearts, and I'll help you. I'll give you wisdom and creativity. I'll teach you to compromise. I'll fill you with courage. I'll give you the strength to persevere."

Building a flourishing marriage has been the most stretching challenge of our lives. It has pressed us into a relationship of dependence on God more than any other challenge we have faced. Our temperaments are so different. Our preferences are so contrary. Our styles are so incongruent. Our patterns are so diverse. Our outlooks are so varied. Our expectations are so conflicting. And while the challenge of meshing our differences has lessened over the years, it certainly hasn't disappeared. We spent the better part of last evening, in fact, struggling over a series of temperament-related hurdles, and went to bed exhausted from the effort.

But we each have so much that the other needs. We help to balance each other's extremes, to cover each other's weaknesses, and to complement each other's strengths. We enrich each other's lives with interests we would not otherwise pursue. We have forced each other to learn tolerance, and then appreciation, for a wide variety of people types; thus we have broadened each other's range of potential friendships, enhanced each other's ministry/career effectiveness, and enabled one another to effectively parent two very different children. Perhaps most importantly, we have prodded one another along the path toward Christlikeness. Each time we have had to crane our necks to look through each other's eyes, or unclench our fists and resist the urge to fight, or prop our elbows on the table and lean forward and say, "I was wrong," we have inched a tiny bit closer to the person we each want to become.

So we wake up each morning thankful for a marriage that challenges but enriches us, and reminds us every day that different isn't bad, it's only different.

Notes

1. Marilyn Bates and David Keirsey, *Please Understand Me* (Del Mar, Calif.: Prometheus Nemesis Book Company, 1984), 17.
2. Ibid., 17.
3. Ibid., 18.
4. *Initiators* and *responders* are our terms. Bob Phillips, author of *The Delicate Art of Dancing with Porcupines*, calls them tellers and askers.
5. Bob Phillips, *The Delicate Art of Dancing with Porcupines* (Ventura, Calif.: Regal Books, 1989).

Seven

Preparing for Conflict

I *don't* believe it."

"It's true. We have been dating for three years and we have never had a fight. What can I say? We were made for each other. What about you two? You've been dating for a long time. What's it been like for you?"

We were more than a little intimidated. How could we sit across the table from the perfect couple and spill the truth about our stormy romance and our broken engagement? Would it hurt to "soften" the story a bit?

"Oh, we've had a few conflicts. But nothing major, and we've always been able to resolve them. Besides, we think it's healthy for dating couples to 'go at it' now and then and learn to work things out. What better way to prepare for marriage?"

"Well, maybe that's true for you. But if we could make it through three years of dating without a problem, I don't see why we should expect trouble in marriage. We won't have the pressures of college, or living with our parents, or juggling part-time jobs. Marriage should be easy compared to what we're dealing with now. It'll be a snap."

We wished them well and left the restaurant thinking that maybe they were right. Maybe marriage *would* be a snap for them. Maybe they could maintain their perfect record. They sure seemed like an ideal match.

But we—and they—were wrong. Establishing careers, maintaining a home, and just living with one another proved to be a bigger challenge than our friends had anticipated. They couldn't figure out how to divide household responsibilities. They discovered they had opposing perspectives on money. In-law tensions put them at odds. Colliding schedules caused frequent angry explosions. Sexual frustrations kept them awake at night. They couldn't agree on vacation plans. . . .

And they desperately needed a vacation! They needed an

escape from reality. After three years of marriage, they felt imprisoned by a solid wall of conflicts they did not know how to resolve. And inside the wall, the air was steaming with the heat of hostility.

EMERGENCY

It is inexcusable that couples are allowed to marry without taking mandatory conflict resolution lessons. Yet it happens all the time. Teachers, pastors, parents, and friends sit idly by and watch starry-eyed lovers overdose on romance and infatuation, knowing full well that eventually reality will strike with a vengeance, conflicts will arise and hostilities brew, and the once blissful couple will face an emergency that neither partner will be prepared to face. Because they have not been coached or trained, they will have no emergency procedures to fall back on.

So what will they do? In most cases, they will resort to the only conflict resolution procedures they are familiar with: the ones their parents used. Even if they witnessed an unhealthy, unacceptable method of conflict resolution, and even if they vowed they would never behave that way, in the absence of proper training, they will almost inevitably revert to the method they grew up with.

Freeze 'Em Out

Some people fall back on the Eskimo style of handling conflict. In a home where this method is used, everyone knows there is a conflict; they can feel it in the air. But nobody talks about it. Everybody backs off, detaches, and mutters under their breath. No matter how large the problem looms, it is never dealt with openly. People negotiate around it, or avoid it, or hope that time will thaw things out. And sometimes the climate does warm up enough for people to start talking again. But the nice weather lasts only until the next conflict, which will probably focus on the same unresolved issue that caused conflict before. In a family like this, nothing is ever really worked through.

In other Eskimo homes the chill never leaves the air. With each new conflict family members add another layer of ice.

Eventually they freeze themselves into total withdrawal from one another.

Let the Bullets Fly

Some families handle conflict cowboy-style. When a problem surfaces or a misunderstanding arises, they square off and start shooting verbal bullets. "This town ain't big enough for the two of us," they announce. Then they shout and throw things and break windows in the saloon. Intimidation is the name of the game. Feelings are ventilated. Anger is released. There is action and drama. But a lot of damage is done along the way. Feelings are hurt and children hear things they should never have to hear.

And the issues that drove people apart remain unresolved.

Let Me Out of Here

Some people deal with conflict by escaping. A family conflict arises, so someone goes out and gets drunk. Another escapist might go on a shopping spree. Somebody else takes drugs. Or walks out for two or three days. Another out is workaholism. The trauma of the self-destructive escapes or the thoughtless disappearing acts tends to cloud the original issue. There is relief when the husband quits drinking or when the wife finally comes home. The problem hasn't been solved, but at least the escapist is home and under control. Until the next conflict.

In escapist families there is plenty of action: doors slamming and people coming and going. But it is conflict avoidance at its best. Issues are never faced, and problems are never solved.

I Don't Know What Happened

Sadly, some people react to conflict by manhandling others. They allow verbal assault to escalate into physical violence, and they create more pain and distance than the original issue could possibly have caused.

Young people who grew up in violent homes usually vow to break that pattern of pain. But too often violence breeds violence. In spite of their good intentions, they resort to what they know. When calamities befall, or frustrations rise, or anger boils, or conflicts rage, or emotions scream for release, they respond reflexively. They lash out; they lose control; they strike.

Later they say, "I don't know what happened. Why did I do that?" The answer is no mystery. In the absence of proper conflict management training, they did the only thing they knew to do. They did what came naturally. The cycle of violence can be broken, but it usually won't be without proper training.

Mandatory Training

Too often relationships that begin with promise end with pain. In the daily rounds of reality, disagreements surface and personalities clash. Harsh words lead to broken trust and hurt feelings. Hidden hostilities choke romance. And a cloud of relational sorrow hangs menacingly overhead. If the pattern continues, the marriage dissolves and another plot is purchased in the relational cemetery.

If we could make this chapter mandatory reading we would. Even the most wisely matched couples will face conflicts in marriage. How they handle them will determine whether their relationship survives or ends up marked with a granite tombstone.

PREREQUISITE FOR SURVIVAL

Most people whose marriages have failed have a ready answer when asked about the demise of their relationship. They blame it on adultery or alcoholism or abuse. They accuse their spouses of dishonesty or insensitivity or irresponsibility. They claim irreconcilable differences or personality conflicts. But such answers don't fit the question. While these factors may cause hurts and disappointments and complications, they are not enough to kill a marriage.

You see, we have witnessed many marriages that have survived the above-mentioned problems. Many have not only survived, but have gone on to flourish. On the other hand, we have known couples who encountered mere tremors of difficulty, but their marriages ended up in the relational graveyard.

What makes the difference? Why are some relationships resistant and resilient and others so susceptible to infection and terminal diseases?

We have observed that in addition to knowing practical tools for conflict resolution, nearly all couples who survive the minor and major conflicts of married life have discovered a key antidote for marital demise. It is called *the spirit of reconciliation*. This elixir produces a heart condition that predisposes people toward reconciliation and revolutionizes the way they approach conflict.

For many people the normal reaction to relational hurt, misunderstanding, or attack is to strike back. To get even. To fix blame. To say, "It's your fault."

We have all behaved that way on occasion. What's more, we have probably felt justified. *What's right is right*, we say. *If you get hurt you gotta get even. I shouldn't have to put up with this. Retaliation is self-preservation.* Then we self-righteously spin on our heels and walk out the slammed door, straight to the relational graveyard. We can't stand the discomfort and turmoil of relational tension, and we see no way to fix it. So we get out the shovel, bury the relationship, and try to get on with life. But we live with a dull, aching pain that won't go away.

Scripture tells us that we were created to live in harmony and community with others. We were created for peace. That is why walking through our relational graveyards causes us so much grief. And why we need to trade in our spirit of retaliation for the spirit of reconciliation.

How do we do that? First, we need to acknowledge that we have fallen short of the moral standards of our holy God and that we are therefore in conflict with Him. Some of us do a pretty good job of not thinking about this, but most of us, during our semiannual moments of introspection, get a little nervous about someday standing before a holy God. We feel a bit uneasy. We sense a latent fear of reprisal or punishment. And we know we can't do anything to escape it. Our past sins won't disappear, and God's holiness won't change. So we are stuck in an unresolvable and unwinnable conflict.

Coming to grips with our desperate position is the first

step toward a spirit of reconciliation. The second step is to realize that God, "being rich in mercy," offered His Son, Jesus Christ, to bridge the chasm of conflict that separates us from God. Through Jesus' death and resurrection, we can be reconciled to God and freed from the fear of condemnation and eternal death. We can be adopted into God's family and relate to Him as a much-loved child relates to a kind father.

The third step toward a reconciling spirit happens naturally to those who have been adopted into God's family and are growing spiritually. The joy of divine reconciliation begins to spill over into other areas of their lives. They want to experience the peace and harmony they enjoy with God with others. They begin to understand that all people—friends, family members, strangers, even enemies—matter to God. The chunks of ice in their chests begin to melt, and they feel concern and compassion for people they previously ignored or spurned or mistreated.

A RADICAL REMAKE

The Bible tells of a wealthy tax collector who routinely ripped people off without the slightest appearance of remorse—until he had a heart-to-heart with Jesus Christ over an unscheduled dinner. After a simple meal and a brief conversation, this hard-hearted extortionist emerged from his house a transformed man. With trembling lips he begged the forgiveness of those he had cheated, and promised to repay them four times over. He even vowed to give half of all his future earnings to the poor.

Obviously something supernatural happened at that dinner table. Not only was a sinner reconciled to God, but he also received the spirit of reconciliation, which turned his feelings toward people upside down. And what happened to Zacchaeus is the norm for all who become reconciled to God. The Holy Spirit plants within them an appreciation for others that wasn't there before. He gives them a longer fuse, more patience, an increased capacity to forgive, a heightened desire for harmony, a sensitivity and tenderness that they never felt before.

B   I know this is true. Before I became reconciled with God, I rarely lost sleep over relational conflicts. If I was

B involved in a private war with somebody, I enjoyed the challenge of making sure I won. If a person claimed to have a problem with me, I assured them that it was their problem. If someone said they didn't like me, I boasted that I didn't care. If I learned I had hurt someone's feelings, I assumed they were overly sensitive. If a relationship seemed destined to die—well, I didn't mind a funeral now and then.

I had a hard heart toward relational problems. I had a spirit of retaliation, of rebellion. I was usually convinced that I was right, and if any doubts surfaced I was quick to submerge them. I was not about to eat crow, or go crawling back on my hands and knees to seek reconciliation.

But then I was broken by an awareness of my sin, and humbled by God's willingness to adopt me into His family. The Holy Spirit began to chip away at my hard heart. "Be tender," he said. "Swallow your pride. Rearrange your values. Be done with hostility. Seek peace. Reconcile."

When the spirit of rebellion reigns in a marriage, every little conflict escalates into a war of harsh accusations. But when the spirit of reconciliation prevails even major conflicts can be discussed constructively and worked through.

After hearing a sermon on reconciliation, a young Marine broke down in tears and said, "Somebody has to lead me to Christ right now. My marriage is in trouble, and I'm sick and tired of trying to fix it on my own. I can't do it. My wife can't do it. We try, but then we get defensive and rebellious. We need to be transformed. We need the spirit of reconciliation. Please help us."

That young couple's marriage was like so many today: destined for the relational graveyard because the wrong spirit prevailed. Some of you may be a bit impatient reading this section. *This is supposed to be a book on marriage*, you say, *not a book on spiritual growth*. But spiritual growth is key to marriage because it is key to the spirit of reconciliation. During our courtship and the early years of our marriage, we were not aware of the practical steps for conflict resolution that we are going to suggest in the next chapter. Had we known them we could have avoided much pain and tension. But at least we both had the spirit of reconciliation. And that kept us working even when the work got so hard, and talking even when the talk seemed to accomplish so little. In spite of our relational difficulties, we refused to rush to the graveyard. Our heart condition drove us toward reconciliation.

It is not enough for one spouse to have a spirit of reconciliation. Both spouses must approach peace negotiations with a willingness to lay down their weapons, admit their mistakes, and work through to a solution. Then they can move successfully through the practical steps to conflict resolution.

Before turning to the next chapter, it may be helpful for you to discuss with your spouse the conflict resolution styles used in the families you grew up in. We also suggest that the two of you talk openly about the spirit of reconciliation. If you don't have it, please reread this chapter and consider becoming reconciled with God. Establishing peace with Him is the most important step you can take, both for you as an individual, and for your marriage.

Eight

Planning Peace Talks

In the previous chapter we mentioned that during the early years of our relationship we were not very good at resolving conflicts. That was a gross understatement. We had the spirit of reconciliation, but absolutely no clue about how to translate that spirit into practical action.

L   I took the Eskimo approach to handling conflict, which fit my introverted temperament perfectly. If Bill did something that hurt or angered me, I registered the offense on my mental tally card and proceeded to freeze him out. I still talked to him, of course, but only when necessary. And I never looked him in the eye, or smiled, or said anything truly pleasant. I pouted. I sighed. I walked around the house looking like my dog had just died.

When Bill asked me what was wrong, I would look at the floor and say, "Nothing."

"Oh, come on," he'd beg. "I know something is wrong. Tell me."

If he pressed hard enough, I would finally reveal my hidden hurt. If he gave up too soon, I'd tuck it deeper inside.

My unwillingness to communicate honestly was very frustrating to Bill. He thought I was being childish, or trying to punish him for offending me. Sometimes he was right, but more often than not I was just confused. I couldn't understand why his behavior bothered me, so I hesitated to mention it. Or I didn't think I was justified in being upset, so I tried to pretend I wasn't. Sometimes I just didn't know how to shape my feelings into words. But regardless of the reason, my failure to communicate openly and clearly often chilled the atmosphere in our home.

L   Bill didn't do much better than I did, though he took the
)   opposite approach. He is by nature a confronter and has
}   little trouble verbalizing his thoughts, so he became a
}   controlled cowboy. He didn't shout or throw things, but
}   he was a sharpshooter with his words. While I insisted on
}   burying anger, he insisted on letting it fly.
       For us, facing conflict became a cultural experience. The
}   cowboy fired his pistol and the Eskimo turned to ice. It was
}   like a Broadway production. But neither of us applauded,
(and both of us got hurt.

It is bad enough that faulty methods of conflict resolution
seldom resolve the conflict. What is worse is that they often
heap hurt upon hurt. A couple expends an enormous amount of
energy trying to work through a problem, and they end up in a
worse state than when they started. Is it any wonder many
couples give up trying to settle their differences?

Many times, in the aftermath of soured conflict negotiations, *we* felt like giving up. But time after time the spirit of
reconciliation prevailed, and instead of giving up we read
another book, or listened to another tape, or talked to another
friend. And eventually we came up with a plan for resolving
conflicts that really works.

IS THAT A PLANK IN YOUR EYE?

The first step in our conflict resolution plan is to pray about
the problem. It is amazing how many insurmountable conflicts
get whittled down to a manageable size in the woodshed of
prayer.

While our human tendency is to cast blame on others and
deny personal guilt, the Holy Spirit has an amazing way of
bringing a more balanced perspective. In the Sermon on the
Mount Jesus challenged His followers to point their fingers at
themselves before pointing them at others. "Why," He asked,
"do you look at the speck of sawdust in your brother's eye and
pay no attention to the plank in your own eye? How can you say
to your brother, 'Let me take the speck out of your eye,' when
all the time there is a plank in your own eye? You hypocrite, first
take the plank out of your own eye, and then you will see clearly
to remove the speck from your brother's eye" (Matt. 7:3–5).

What does this say to spouses? It tells us that every time we feel slighted, offended, taken advantage of, or hurt, before we take out the guns and start shooting, or run away, or freeze someone out, we need to get alone with God and ask some probing questions. *Am I the problem here? Am I being unreasonable or selfish or insensitive? Am I aggravating the situation? Am I yielding to sin?*

We can each recall numerous times when we thought the other was totally out of line. We were each convinced that the evidence was on our side. One wore the white hat and the other the black. But so often in prayer our eyes were opened to an entirely different picture. We became aware of false assumptions we had been making. Of judgmental attitudes we had been harboring. Of impatience. Of insensitivity. Of intolerance. So many times we have been on the verge of "straightening each other out," only to find that we were the ones who needed to be straightened out. With God's help, each of us has resolved many so-called marital conflicts without ever having to involve our spouse.

We believe that the tension in most marriages could be cut in half if spouses would pray every day about their marriages. God does miracles when people pray. Lives are changed and hearts softened when people pray. Pointing fingers change direction when people pray. Problems shrink when people pray. Sometimes, conflicts even disappear when people pray.

L   Many years ago, Bill and I decided to set aside Thursday night as our date night. However, more often than not, Bill ended up with a scheduling conflict, and I ended up spending our date night alone. I was tempted to accuse Bill of being careless, but as I prayed about the problem, I realized we had simply chosen a bad time. For a pastor, evening hours are the hardest hours to protect. I suggested that we move our date "night" to Thursday morning and see what happened. It worked. Because we are both morning people, we have actually enjoyed Thursday mornings more than we ever enjoyed Thursday nights. God's idea was much better than ours.

So, before you go to your spouse, go to God. See what wisdom and insight He has to offer.

CAN WE TALK?

The next step is to plan a formal peace conference in a quiet, unrushed setting where you and your spouse can face the issue head on.

"Come on," you say, "don't sell us short. We talk about our marriage problems. I pass through the family room and give a few shots. My spouse nags and complains at the dinner table. We may get a little sarcastic, a little small now and then. But we know what the issues are. We know how to go after each other."

Maybe you do know what the issues are. But there is a big difference between "going after each other" and really solving problems. We have found that serious conflict can seldom be worked out in the cracks of life. You can't do it on the run, or when the kids are climbing all over you, or as you are drifting off to sleep at night. You need to plan a peace conference in a neutral setting when you both have optimal energy.

It is also important to schedule peace talks as soon as possible. Paul says, "Do not let the sun go down while you are still angry" (Eph. 4:26). His words suggest daily peace talks for conflicts that have arisen in the course of that day. Busy schedules sometimes make that impossible, and serious issues may require more formally scheduled peace talks, but even those should be scheduled as soon as possible. In the meantime, couples must covenant together not to "sin in their anger." They must both refrain from the kind of "cheap shots"—sarcasm, innuendo, and rudeness—that inevitably complicate the issues. We call this delicate period of time between recognizing a problem and resolving it "the commitment phase," and we will discuss it more in a later chapter.

Often, a portion of our Thursday morning date is devoted to a peace talk. We go to a local restaurant, sit in a booth in a dark, secluded corner, and spread the issues out on the table. Resolving conflicts has a remarkable way of draining relational tension and drawing people together, so by the time we finish the peace talk we are usually in a great mood to enjoy the rest of the morning.

People who are night people should plan their peace talks over a quiet dinner. Others would do well to schedule lunch appointments. If you have small children, we suggest hiring a baby-sitter or trading baby-sitting services with a friend, so your peace talks can be unrushed and undisturbed.

But let's say you have scheduled the peace talk and you are seated across the table from one another. Now what?

Begin with Affirmation

We used to jump right into the problem, which meant we were starting the discussion from a negative position. Doing that almost always polarized us and elicited defensive responses.

Learning to begin with affirmation helped us start our discussions from a positive position. Doing that softened the blow of the conflict and kept us from reeling into defensiveness. Our peace talks became much more peaceful when we learned to say, "Honey, I love you and I am committed to our marriage. But I think it can be better than it is. Here are some ideas I have."

An introduction like that can lead to a constructive conversation.

Be Willing to Take Blame

Bring to the meeting the insights and attitudes that were fostered during your time of private prayer. Acknowledge specifically how you contributed to the tension. Do not take blame you don't deserve, but fully accept what is rightly yours.

"I should never have said what I said."

"I'm sorry I was so selfish."

"Forgive me for letting my ego get in the way."

"I feel horrible about blowing up in front of the kids."

"I've been expecting too much from you."

"It was unfair for me to think you could read my mind."

"I didn't communicate clearly. I'm sorry I misled you."

You will be amazed at the power of apology. Two short words—I'm sorry—have saved business partnerships, reconciled neighbors, reunited fathers and sons, and rescued marriages that were headed for the graveyard. There is no magic in the words themselves, but when they are said sincerely they reveal what is underneath—the spirit of reconciliation. And they open up the lines of communication.

When Zacchaeus, the reformed tax collector, ran out into the streets, the people who knew him probably ran in the opposite direction. "How is he going to cheat us this time?" they wondered. "What new scam has he concocted?" But apparently he stopped them dead in their tracks. How? He said, "I'm sorry. I was wrong. I cheated you. I want to make it right." They were probably suspicious; they probably had a wait-and-see attitude. But like most people, they wanted to believe the best. So they listened. They opened their hearts. And Zacchaeus' apology opened the way for healing and restitution.

Express Hurt Instead of Hostility

Most problems start with hurt. A wife feels hurt because her husband didn't ask about a presentation she made at work that day. Or because he forgot their anniversary. Or was unnecessarily critical of her mother. A husband feels hurt because his wife didn't notice the weight he lost. Or because she wasn't sensitive about a pressure at work. Or she insulted him in front of a friend.

Hurt is a legitimate response to disappointment and offense, and it should never be denied or kept hidden inside. It should always be expressed and discussed. But hurt becomes a problem when people let it build up inside and turn into anger. The wife starts out being hurt by her husband's apparent lack of interest in her career, but after she mulls the hurt around in her mind for a while it becomes infected. She ends up being angry at "the insensitive louse who only cares about what he does."

This is why it is important to plan peace talks as soon as possible, before hurt turns to anger. Most people are moved by another person's pain, so revealing hurt can build bridges of understanding and compassion. But ventilating hostility blows up bridges, because people are repelled by angry assaults. When someone attacks, our natural reaction is to fight back.

Another mistake that causes hurt to turn to anger is accumulating grievances. One hurt is manageable. You can keep it under control, express it constructively, and work through it.

Two hurts are a little harder to deal with. Accumulate more than that and it is almost impossible to keep them from comparing notes and deciding that they deserve to turn into anger.

During the early years of our marriage we repeatedly accumulated piles of grievances. Eventually we became so full of anger we exploded and said all kinds of destructive things. Even Eskimos can reach the boiling point if the hidden hurts simmer long enough.

So please deal with grievances as they arise. Don't stack them on top of one another or let them fester inside until they turn to hostility. Anger is always a secondary emotion. If spouses back up to what preceded it, they will often find hurt. If they reveal the hurt, they will weaken the walls that separate them.

Make Direct Statements

Hints and offhand remarks accomplish little. Whether we are in the midst of a formal peace talk or a casual conversation, we must say what we mean.

L   I don't know why, but I had a hard time with this one. It was much easier for me to say, "It sure has been a long, busy day. What a drag to have to cook dinner tonight," than to say, "Bill, I have had a rough day and I don't have the energy to cook dinner. I would really like to go out tonight." Of course, if Bill didn't pick up on my hint and suggest that we go out for dinner, I thought he was insensitive and unconcerned about my needs.

I had to work hard on stating my desires and frustrations honestly and clearly. During peace talks, that means saying, "I was upset because you didn't call to tell me you would be late," rather than saying, "I think husbands should be more respectful of their wives' schedules." I need to own my thoughts and feelings and express them in specific terms. It is much easier for us to deal with something honest and concrete like my disappointment about Bill not calling me, than to deal with a vague generality about husbands and wives and respect.

Make "I Feel" Statements

Many peace plans are sabotaged by *you* statements of accusation that antagonize spouses and often terminate the peace process before it even starts.

"You don't help enough around the house."

"You spend too much time at work."

"You don't know how to handle money."

"You are insensitive."

I feel statements are much less inflammatory and open the door for further discussion and practical problem solving.

"I feel overwhelmed by household responsibilities. I have thought of some ways we might be able to divide up the tasks. Can I tell you about them?"

"I often feel left out of your life because you spend so much time at work. Can we talk about that?"

"I feel frustrated about our financial situation. Would you be willing to discuss some ways to keep our budget in better order?"

"I felt hurt by your comments this morning. You probably didn't mean to offend me, but let me tell you how I felt."

Avoid "Never" and "Always"

L   I am an extremist. To me there is no middle ground. Life is black or white, happy or sad, up or down, wonderful or terrible. Unfortunately, this perspective tends to color my communication patterns. Too often I speak in exaggerated terms.

"You never come home on time."

"You always forget to call."

"You are forever leaving dirty dishes in the family room."

I may have a perfectly reasonable concern, but if I express it in extreme terms, I invalidate it. I turn the truth into a lie. Does Bill *never* come home on time? Does he *always* forget to call? Is he *forever* leaving dirty dishes in the family room? Well ... about the dishes.

If we want our grievances to be taken seriously we must make accurate, truthful, realistic statements. *Always* and *never* will always—well, almost always—shift the focus away from the real issue. The unreasonably accused spouse will probably dismiss the original concern and blame the relational tension on the other spouse's poor communication techniques.

I HAVE AN IDEA!

So, come to the peace talks with a spirit of reconciliation. Affirm your relationship and be quick to say, "I'm sorry." Express hurts instead of hostilities. And make direct, realistic "I feel" statements.

Then commit yourself to being solution centered. A husband once told us, "Well, I did what you suggested. I took my wife out for a peace talk. But it didn't help. I told her what I thought; she told me what she thought. Then we went home with our basket load of accusations. What good did that do?" It did no good because they weren't solution centered. They each presented their case and hoped the other would give in. A better approach would have been to sit down at the table and ask, "How can we compromise? How can we adjust and adapt? What would be a mutually satisfactory alternative?"

If spouses have spent time in prayer prior to the meeting, they probably already have possible options in mind, or even listed on paper. They can bring these ideas to the peace talk, not as definite answers to the problem, but as starting points, as possibilities to be reshaped and refined together.

We used to argue over money. "Why did you spend money on *that*?" "But I thought we were saving for *this*." "You said we had to be frugal this month, and now look what you bought." Finally we decided we needed to agree on a yearly budget. So we prayed for flexibility and open-mindedness, then sat down and hammered out a budget that we signed and vowed to stick with. Every January we update and revise it, and we haven't had a serious budgeting conflict in years.

We had similar conversations regarding scheduling. Because our schedules were so imbalanced during the early years of our marriage, we both experienced major hurt and frustration in this area. Eventually we had to work out a plan detailing how many nights we could be gone each week, how much traveling we could do, when we should schedule our weekly date, and what to do when scheduling commitments overlap. Establishing mutually agreed upon guidelines freed us from constant disagreements and disappointments.

MOMENT OF TRUTH

We have discovered that problems which caused either of us a high degree of hurt in the past, or problems that require complex solutions, have the potential to bring out the worst in us, even during peace talks. In such cases, we have to work very hard not to undermine the peace process.

B   During one particularly difficult discussion, Lynne and I were following the steps for conflict resolution as best we could, but a resolution was not coming easily. No leaflet had dropped from heaven with a three-point plan printed on it. No ideas were popping full-blown into our minds. We were both beginning to realize that we felt more strongly than we had thought about the items on our individual agendas. We were trying to compromise, but we were both being stretched—farther than we had anticipated.

Eventually, pride started to surface, evil forces began to rear their ugly heads, and the dark side of my humanity decided to play its card. Flashing across the screen of my imagination was a scene from a television movie I had just seen. A husband and wife were faced off in a heated verbal assault. The lights cast a sinister glow, the camera zoomed in, the music built to a crescendo, and at the height of emotional intensity, the husband blasted his wife with deadly words, turned on his heels, and left the room— slamming the door behind him. That image flashed on my mental screen and I thought, *That's what I want to do! It would feel so good to let loose a verbal barrage and slam a door*.

But I knew that while that kind of behavior makes for good Nielsen ratings, it makes for bad marriages. On top of that, it's a cowardly response to conflict. It takes far more courage to fight pride and evil desires than it takes to fight my wife. When you're in the thick of battle, it's so easy to be a jerk. It's so easy to let your frustrations fly, to

B give free rein to your anger, to be petty and immature. But
those times are moments of truth. Inside you want to be
childish, you want the easy way out, you want to win. But
the Holy Spirit is cheering for you to do what's right:
"Control yourself. Stick with the process. Don't deny your
feelings, but express them constructively. Negotiate. Compromise. Reconcile." Who you listen to in those moments
of decision reveals your character and courage.

I've heard men say, "I had a fight with the old lady. Boy,
did I tell her. . . ." And I think, *Do you really believe it takes
valor to leave a peace talk, slam a door, and then brag about it
to your friends? Do you really think I'm impressed?*

What takes courage is to stay at the table and say, "We
made an inch of progress today. Maybe tomorrow we can
move forward another inch. But we won't give up until we
solve this problem."

WOULD YOU HELP US, PLEASE?

But what if your peace talks aren't working? What if you
can't stay on track? What if you constantly go forward one inch
and back two? The next step is to seek counsel from a trusted
friend or couple. Proverbs 11:14 says, "For lack of guidance a
nation falls, but many advisers make victory sure." We shudder
to think where we would be without the wise, insightful, and
sometimes painful counsel we have received from trusted
friends.

We are not talking here about golf buddies or bridge
partners. Nor do we advocate gossip sessions where one spouse
complains about the other. We are talking about trusted and
respected friends, and about constructive conversations in which
we seek counsel not about our spouse's behavior, but about our
own.

B   A close friend once told me, "You're too frugal with
your wife. You're liberal when it comes to giving to God's
work. You're liberal with your kids. You're liberal when
your friends are in need. But you're pretty cheap with your
wife. You need to be more generous with her."

B Another friend said, "You're more demanding with your wife than you think you are. You expect too much from her. You need to give her a little slack."

One said, "You ought to take more interest in your house and yard. You enjoy having an orderly, well-maintained refuge to come home to, but you don't take enough responsibility for keeping it that way."

I didn't like hearing those things, but I needed to hear them. They were true, and they were building walls in my relationship with Lynne. I'm thankful I had friends who knew me and loved me enough to take the risk of telling me the truth. And I'm thankful that I had learned the value of accepting hard counsel.

We have also benefited from seeking counsel together from another couple. "What advice can you give us about this situation?" we ask. "How do you compromise in this area? How have you solved this problem?" At times we have had to schedule formal peace talks with our friends. Sometimes we just use casual get-togethers as opportunities to glean insight from married couples we respect.

CALL IN THE PROFESSIONALS

But what if you haven't established accountable relationships with friends? What if there are no couples with whom you both feel comfortable sharing? Or what if they have tried to help you, but they can't? Then please go to a counselor.

For the most part, contemporary Americans are counsel-crazy. We think nothing of hiring a consultant to help with management problems, or an accountant to help with finances. We don't hesitate to take our medical problems to doctors or our legal questions to lawyers. We willingly go to nutritionists for dietary advice, and to color analysts to find out how we should dress. But if someone suggests going to a marriage counselor we say, "In a hearse, I'll go! I can handle my household. I don't need help. Not me. No way."

Some people refuse to seek counsel because they are embarrassed; they don't want anyone to know their marriage is a bit frayed around the edges. Some people refuse because they are afraid to face a painful truth, or afraid of what they might learn about themselves or their spouse. Others refuse because they are stubborn and cruel. They would rather dismantle the emotional health of their spouse than expend the energy to get help. Still others question the theological "rightness" of seeking professional counsel. "Shouldn't we be able to pray ourselves out of this problem? Shouldn't we be able to find an answer in the Bible?"

We believe that prayer and Bible study are important elements in marital health. We also believe, however, that God has gifted certain individuals with a degree of discernment, knowledge, and wisdom that allows them to assist couples who occasionally hit impasses, or couples who are stuck in unhealthy, destructive patterns of relating.

Some couples get stuck for so long they forget what a good marriage is like. They begin to settle for a mediocre marriage, or even for a miserable one. They need somebody to refresh their minds and teach them how to get back to a healthy, positive, loving way of relating.

Sometimes only one spouse is willing to seek counsel. We encourage that partner to go alone. It is better for one partner to get unstuck than for both to remain where they are. We have seen God do amazing things through one spouse who is willing to face the challenge of growth. Many times the unwilling spouse is impacted by the visible change in the other.

Conflict resolution requires courage and persistence. It calls for humility and honesty. It chips away at our hardness of heart, and sometimes it produces pain. But it is always worth whatever effort it takes, whatever inconvenience it causes, and whatever change or compromise it requires.

Nine

Whatever Happened to Romance?

Several years into our marriage a casual conversation with a male acquaintance awakened me to a serious problem in our marriage. Over lunch in a local restaurant Bill and I listened while this middle-aged consultant for an international manufacturing firm lamented having to spend so much time away from his wife.

"I make the best of it though," he said. "I call her every night and we talk about what happened during the day. I send her lots of little notes and cards, just to remind her I'm thinking about her. If I travel to interesting places I buy her jewelry that is representative of the area. And I always come home with lingerie—something fun and flirtatious that puts us in the mood for romance. We have to be apart so often, we want to make the time we have together count!"

He mentioned his wife several other times during the conversation, and it became obvious that after twenty-five years of marriage he was still "crazy in love" with her. He still treasured her. He still looked forward to being with her. He still had fun with her. He still got a kick out of making love to her.

As I listened, I found myself being strangely attracted to this man, and it frightened me. I didn't understand it. There I was, sitting next to my handsome, successful young husband to whom I was wholeheartedly committed. Yet I was feeling drawn to a fiftyish grandfather who talked nonstop about his wife. What was going on?

Throughout the afternoon I pondered the conversation and finally realized that the reason I felt drawn to that man was that I longed to be loved and treasured the way he

L loved and treasured his wife. I wanted to feel special, to be pursued, to know that my husband delighted in me—and that wasn't happening in our marriage at that point.

It is happening in our marriage now, and you will see how the change came about in the next chapter. But before the romantic rebirth of our marriage, Bill and I had many difficult conversations. The evening of our talk with the businessman, I described for Bill what I had felt during lunch and what I had learned during the afternoon.

"I love you, Bill, and I am more committed to our marriage than I have ever been. But we've lost something along the way. Our marriage seems more like a business, a partnership, a joint venture, than like an intimate, loving union. We struggle along, trying to live in peace as best we can, but there is too little spark in our relationship. Too little fun. Too little romance. I don't want to go on like this anymore. Marriage should be so much more than this. We should be so much happier than we are. We need to get the romance back."

We need to get the romance back. We have heard so many spouses make that statement. Couples who are unhappy with their marriages often admit that what disturbs them more than anything is the lack of romance. *If I married the right person*, a spouse asks, *why did the courtship end so abruptly after the wedding? Why did the flames die so quickly? Why is there so much less "feeling" in our marriage than there used to be?*

Few couples expect to maintain the intense, supercharged, adolescent-style relationship that marked the height of their courtship. In fact, most couples feel somewhat relieved when life begins to settle into a more normal routine, and they can get about the tasks of real life again. But many marriages settle down too much. Within a few short years the sparkle has faded completely. Feelings have become mere memories. Romance has become something to read about in cheap novels. Spouses relate like roommates who share an occasional one-night stand. And together they face thirty more years of disappointment and frustration.

WHAT PULLS THE PLUG ON ROMANCE?

A number of factors drain the romance out of marriage. One is the curse of familiarity. It happens in all arenas of life. You buy a new car and for a few weeks you create reasons to go to the store so you can drive it. You wash it on lunch break. You make your kids shower before they get near it. But after a while, without even realizing it, you begin treating your new car the way you treated the old one. You let the dog crawl around in it. You let the kids drink milk shakes in it. You say, "I don't have to worship this. It's just a car."

The same thing happens when you buy a new house, a new piece of furniture, or a new item of clothing. For a while you treat it so carefully, but once the shine wears off and the glitter fades—once familiarity sets in—you quit protecting it and worrying about it and caring for it so meticulously.

Unfortunately, we often treat people the same way we treat purchases. During the courtship phase, when a guy arrives to pick up his girlfriend for a date, he barely touches the doorbell before the door swings wide open and she says, "Oh Tom, I've been thinking about you all day. I've been counting the ticks of the clock. I thought you would never arrive." After two years of marriage, Tom comes home from work forty-five minutes late and announces, "I'm home, honey." His wife says, "So am I. What do you want, a marching band?"

A twisted sense of security can also drain the romance out of marriage. During the courtship phase, partners live with the nagging fear that if they don't stay on their toes, if they aren't thoughtful and courteous, if they don't communicate creatively, if they don't "beat the competition," they might lose the relationship. Once they are married, however, some people get a little too complacent. They feel a little too secure. They get careless, thoughtless, and matter-of-fact about their relationship.

Physical exhaustion can also drain the romance out of marriage. When do most people have their highest levels of energy? During their late teens and early twenties—when they are courting. So with time and boundless energy their romance flourishes. They go out on dates five nights a week. Stay up talking till 2 A.M. Schedule breakfast meetings before dawn so they can watch the sunrise. Many college couples do what we did. As soon as the young man's Friday afternoon class ends, he jumps in his car and drives fourteen hours to his girlfriend's college, where he spends a day and a half with her before driving back to his campus for his Monday morning class. The next weekend she visits him.

But few couples can maintain that pace over the long haul. During the coming years their energy levels seem to plummet. One beautiful summer evening (the kind they used to think was created for romance), after they put the kids to bed at 8 P.M., the young wife halfheartedly suggests they take a walk around the block.

"Are you kidding?" says her weary husband. "I feel like I'm dead on my feet already, and I have to be at the office at 6 A.M."

"Yeah, I know. I feel the same way, and the baby will probably be up again in a few hours. Maybe some other time."

What really complicates things is that at the same time their energy drops, their responsibilities skyrocket. Career. Kids. Car pools. The PTA. The handyman special they call a house. In-law challenges. Church involvement. Community service. And then they look in the mirror and notice that their bodies need a little attention, so they try to squeeze in some exercise.

In addition to increased responsibility and time commitments, there is often an increased financial burden. During courtship many young people live with parents or roommates and have minimal living expenses. So they have plenty of excess money to spend on dates. One young man told us about renting a tux to wear to take his girlfriend out for dinner—just for fun. We thought, *Wait till that guy gets married. Wait till he's making house payments and buying cars and furniture. And wait till he's raising kids.* Kids are fun, but they are costly little critters. His wife is going to suggest a quiet, get-away dinner, and he is going to break his arm patting himself on the back for wearing a three-year-old sport jacket. His tux days are going to seem like a lifetime away. Who thinks about long-stemmed roses and romantic dinners when you need a crib, a lawn mower, and a new roof?

As the years pass, life gets more and more complicated. What usually takes the brunt of all the madness? Marriage. *He can wait. She will understand. We'll attend to the marriage later, when we have more time and more energy and more creativity and more money.*

But that seldom happens. Why? Because while all of these complicating factors are entering the marriage picture, there is something even more sinister going on beneath the surface of too many marriages. We have discovered that many marriages that are short on romance have arrived at that unpleasant spot via a common route. Though the coming illustration focuses primarily on a husband's error in judgment, more and more wives are making the same mistake.

TOP PRIORITY

The journey begins like this. A young man identifies the woman he wants to marry and begins the business of serious courtship. Time and money are no object, so he throws vast amounts of energy and creativity into the pursuit. He gives gifts, sends cards, writes poems, delivers flowers, plans romantic dinners in elegant restaurants, takes long walks on sandy beaches, enjoys leisurely drives on country roads, and loiters in front of glittering jewelry store windows. He is on a mission. He has a worthy goal. He is motivated. He lets nothing stand in the way of winning the woman of his dreams. She becomes his top priority, and he will not rest until she is his.

He is smitten and he wants her to know it. He rearranges his busy schedule to spend every possible minute with her. He compliments her warmly. He sings her praises to friends and family. He talks about her constantly. And very slowly he begins to wear her down.

That's right, wear her down. You see, she was a little suspicious at first. He was obviously in hot pursuit, but what exactly did that mean? What was he after? Did he want a cheap thrill or a lasting relationship? A female trophy or a wife he could treasure? She knows the dangers because she has been hurt before. So she wisely guards her heart and maintains her distance. She observes, waits, and analyzes. Can this guy be trusted? Or will he dash her dreams six months after the wedding? She has heard the horror stories, and doesn't intend to provide the plot for another one.

Meanwhile, the diligent young man showers her with

attention, affection, and appreciation. He calls her four times a day, fills her mailbox with declarations of love, and buys her sentimental gifts and exotic perfumes. The weekends are wall-to-wall recreation and romance: dinners, movies, plays, parties. And now—the offer of a diamond ring.

Almost against her will, she feels loved. She feels safe and secure and treasured and prized and wanted. She begins to trust him. She begins to believe that it will last. In fact, she lets herself believe that it will keep getting better and better, and that marriage will open the door to a future of unimagined joy.

Finally, the last bridge of doubt is crossed and she says, "Yes, yes, I will marry you. You have proven beyond a shadow of doubt that you love me. You have courted me, romanced me, made me feel special and important and treasured. You have convinced me that I am at the top of your priority list. You have won my heart. I will marry you!"

So the wedding date is set, the ceremony is carefully planned, and the honeymoon is arranged. It all comes off in storybook style. The newly married couple move into their cozy studio apartment and the young wife settles into the realities of everyday married life, reveling in the knowledge that she made a wise and wonderful choice for a lifetime partner.

I GOT THAT JOB DONE!

And then it happens. Her husband does a terrible, horrible, awful, unthinkable, rotten, reprehensible thing. Oh, he doesn't realize he is doing anything wrong. But he does it, nonetheless, and deeply wounds his sincere, trusting wife.

What does he do? He shifts gears. He readjusts his focus. He figures that now that he got the "marriage job" done it is time to move on to another objective. He faced one challenge and beat it; now it is time to face another one. So without giving one thought to how this is going to impact his wife, he calmly rearranges his priorities, reapportions his energies, and launches out on his next mission, most likely in the marketplace.

There is no malice in his decision. In fact, he is probably not even aware that he is making the shift. If questioned about his love for his wife, he would deny that it has faltered in the least. He loves her as much as he did the day he married her. He is simply doing what he has been conditioned to do.

It goes all the way back to childhood. Dad assigns the little guy a list of responsibilities and says, "Now, you do this chore, and when you complete it satisfactorily, then you move on to the next chore, and you continue till you work your way down the list." So the little guy does exactly as he is told. He completes one chore, then shifts his focus to the next one. When he gets older and becomes involved in athletics, he learns quickly how the system works. First there are the tryouts; then the practices and the games; finally, the tournaments and the award banquets. Then you put that uniform away, and three weeks later you shift your focus to the next sport.

It is the same in the marketplace. He receives an assignment from his manager and is told to work on it, complete it, and then present it. After he does that, he packs up and moves to the next assignment. This *modus operandi*, this task-oriented approach, becomes a way of life for many men, and it extends right into their relational lives. Marriage seems to fit the pattern perfectly. They pour their efforts into courtship, get the marriage job done, and attend the award banquet—the honeymoon. Then they move on to the next job, the next task, the next challenge.

Not all men do this, of course. But it is not uncommon. Many men are raised this way, and without giving it a moment's thought, they function this way. It comes naturally for them and makes perfect sense. "Yeah," a man says, "I do operate that way. What's the big deal? It's interesting, but far from earth-shattering."

A NIGHTMARE COME TRUE

Unfortunately, it *is* earth-shattering to the unsuspecting, trusting woman he married. Throughout the courtship she had been leery. She had questioned and analyzed. But he had been so tenacious, so convincing. Finally, she gave in. She let herself feel treasured. And now, just as she sits poised with pen in hand, preparing to write the story on wedded bliss, her husband closes the book so he can focus on a new agenda. He wants to make a buck or two. Or climb a rung or two. Or build a church or two.

And he works so hard he no longer has the time or energy for love letters or long walks or candlelight dinners or flowers or phone calls or back rubs or three-hour conversations about building a life together. Those were front-burner issues back when he was trying to get the marriage job done, but now it's done. To complicate matters, he convinces himself that the best way to show love for his wife is to provide well for her. So, with even greater abandon, he throws himself into his work.

The young wife is devastated. Her worst nightmare is coming true. She views his refocus of attention as evidence of personal rejection. "I guarded my heart for two and a half years," she cries. "And then I let myself be fooled. I bought hook, line, and sinker into all the wining, dining, and courting. And now here I sit. I was duped. Set up. How could I have been so stupid?"

Sometimes the husband's behavior wipes out his wife's self-esteem. Sometimes it just makes her angry. Either way, it convinces her that she married the wrong man.

We recently attended a small conference with a number of couples in the fifty- to sixty-year age range. We observed that many of the men were unusually attentive toward their wives. Because we were in the midst of working on this book, we asked them why. Almost without exception, the men said, "This is my second wife. During my first marriage I was too preoccupied with climbing the corporate ladder to pay attention to my wife. I hurt her deeply for many years, and finally she couldn't take it anymore. Now I'm doing things differently. I may have forfeited my first wife, but I'm not going to foul things up again."

Most men don't intend to hurt their wives. They do what they do without thinking. And, as we mentioned earlier, husbands aren't the only ones who fall into this pattern. The unprecedented entrance of women into the marketplace has put wives at equal risk when it comes to refocusing their energies and neglecting romance. In many marriages nowadays, both spouses make the destructive shift. A young couple we know were best friends all through high school, dated happily throughout college, and married with the total blessing of family and friends. But five years into marriage they sat across from one another on their living room floor, weeping over the lack of feeling in their marriage. They weren't spiritually incompatible. They hadn't lost respect for one another. They didn't have serious temperament clashes or poor conflict resolution skills. They had simply poured themselves into their careers and neglected to treasure one another.

While some people let their careers get in the way of romance, others get sidetracked by parenting. They get so caught up in child-rearing responsibilities that they forget they are husbands and wives first, parents second. In attempting to give their best to their children, they fail to give them what they need most: a happily married mom and dad.

WOULDN'T IT BE NICE ...

"How are things going at home?"

"How are you and your wife getting along?"

"How is your relationship with your husband?"

Too often the responses to such questions reveal a less-than-happy state of affairs.

"Well, uh, not bad, tolerable. You know how it goes."

"Oh, all right. I suppose it could be better."

"You asked me at a bad time."

Wouldn't it be nice if more couples could answer those questions like this:

"We're having a great time. Our marriage is better than ever."

"I'm nuts about my wife. I love being with her."

"I'm crazy about my husband. We have so much fun together."

Wouldn't it be nice to see more husbands and wives finding great delight in one another? And developing soul companionship with one another? And deepening their lifelong commitments to one another? Wouldn't it be nice to see more couples modeling a tremendous marriage so their kids will know what to aim for when they get married? Wouldn't it be nice to see romance taking its rightful place in marriage?

Some people think that the only way to get romance back in their marriage is to get into a different marriage. But many people who opt out of a romanceless marriage find themselves, two or three years later, in another romanceless marriage. They thought they needed a new partner, but what they really needed was a new pattern of relating and expressing love. They thought they needed a new marriage, but what they really needed was a new motivation for rekindling their old one.

OUR JOURNEY BACK

B One thing that really bothered me during the early years of our marriage was that Lynne kept pushing to build a great marriage. She wanted our marriage to be out of the ordinary. She had lofty goals regarding oneness and companionship and romance. She was committed to pursuing an ideal marriage.

I, like many people, was content with a mediocre marriage. Five on a ten scale was fine with me. I loved Lynne and was committed to the institution of marriage, but I couldn't see being preoccupied with marriage when there were so many other things to be concerned about. I was busy building a church. I was busy developing a staff. I was busy leading people to Christ. I was busy trying to make the house payment. I was busy trying to be a great father to my kids. I was busy, I tell you! I couldn't figure out why Lynne was so bound and determined to set such lofty and time-consuming goals for our relationship. Though I never verbally condemned her expectations, I made my position known in a thousand nonverbal ways. I was more than willing to settle for average.

I tried to convince myself that it was a time problem, that I didn't have enough hours in my day to build a great marriage. But it was really a motivation problem. I did not have an inner drive to build my marriage.

At sixteen, when I became a Christian, I knew that Jesus Christ had done for me what I couldn't do for myself— purchased my eternal salvation. And I was determined to express my gratitude by obeying His commandments and serving Him diligently. One of the first verses I memorized was Colossians 3:23, "Whatever you do, work at it with all your heart, as working for the Lord, not for men."

I knew I fell far short, but I was sincere and kept striving. I nurtured my daily walk with Jesus Christ wholeheartedly.

B I devoted myself to my ministry wholeheartedly. I developed and used my spiritual gifts wholeheartedly. I pursued purity and love in my friendships wholeheartedly. I committed myself to fatherhood wholeheartedly.

But in my relationship with my wife, I was halfhearted. I don't remember why. Maybe I didn't know how to be wholehearted in marriage. Maybe I was overwhelmed by the challenge. Maybe I truly thought a mediocre marriage was all God had in mind for us. For whatever the reason, I applied a different standard to marriage.

In nearly every other area of my life I was disciplined and goal oriented, and I sought to please and honor God. But in my marriage I was undisciplined, I had established low goals, and I failed to view marital growth as a matter of obedience. As a result, I saw examples of divine intervention and supernatural blessing in every area of my life except my relationship with Lynne.

Eventually the contrast between what was happening in my marriage and what was happening in the rest of my life—and the chastising words of some close friends who observed my behavior toward Lynne—kicked some sense into me. I finally took off the marital blinders and noticed what the Bible had to say to husbands. In Ephesians 5:25, Paul tells husbands to "treasure your wives." A Greek verb study revealed that the present imperative tense was used in this verse. So a more accurate translation would be: "Husbands, *keep on treasuring* your wives." That verse hit me like a bulldozer. I wasn't treasuring Lynne. I had shifted gears with the best of 'em. I had gotten the marriage job done and moved on to new challenges. I was blatantly violating God's command.

First Peter 3:7 tells husbands to "be considerate as you live with your wives, and treat them with respect." I wasn't doing that. I wasn't being sensitive toward Lynne. I wasn't showing her courtesy or honor or respect. At least not wholeheartedly.

I don't know why I had been so blind before, but when I finally started seeing clearly, I decided to do something about it. I have to confess that I was not at that point motivated by my feelings for Lynne. Though I was

B committed to her and to our marriage, my gear-shifting routine had wounded her so deeply that she had become hostile and cold. Because I didn't understand what had caused her to become that way, I responded with anger and impatience and frustration. So the tension between us was high, the warmth was low, and there was little on a feeling level to motivate me to move toward her.

What did motivate me was the sudden realization that being totally devoted to my wife—and to rekindling our marriage—was part of my commitment to God.

Since the day I became a Christian I have longed to hear God say someday, "Well done, Bill. You have served Me faithfully. You have obeyed Me conscientiously. You have pleased Me in your personal walk with Me, in your ministry, in your teaching, in your financial management, in your parenting, in your friendships, in how you have treated your body. Well done. Thank you for trusting Me. Thank you for standing strong for Me."

Now I wanted to add my marriage to the list. I wanted to be able to hear someday, "Well done, Bill. You have been a godly husband. You kept on treasuring your wife." So I vowed to become devoted to Lynne, to begin treasuring her the way I was supposed to. And I promised to do it even if she didn't make a reciprocal commitment.

As it turned out, that was a good thing. By the time I made this covenant with God, it was almost too late for Lynne. She had been so wounded by my neglect that she responded to my dramatic turnaround with little more than indifference for nearly two years. That was extremely frustrating for me, but it did not undermine my commitment to wholeheartedness, because my motivation was not centered on Lynne's response. I learned that God is faithful to give us the strength and courage we need to make the changes required by obedience. And my obedience freed us to take the long journey back to romance.

HEALTHY OPTIONS

And it *was* a long journey. Closing the book on romance had done so much damage to our relationship that we were beyond the help of a quick cure. In retrospect, however, we see ways that we could have minimized the damage and shortened the healing process.

L   Early in our marriage I tried to call for help and express my hurt. I tried to tell Bill that I felt neglected, like the last item on his priority list, and that I sensed us drifting apart. But he didn't see it. He thought I was being unreasonable. So he refused to change.

Eventually my hurt turned to anger, and I alternated between sullen withdrawal and hateful outbursts. Both reactions drove Bill deeper into his work and further away from romance. Why, he asked himself, should he come home to a wife who was detached one day, and openly antagonistic the next? In his work, he was successful and productive; he received affirmation; he spent his day with pleasant people. At home, he felt judged and condemned, and daily faced an unhappy wife. Had he not been convicted by the Word of God, he would probably never have reopened the book on romance and made marriage the priority it is supposed to be.

Bill was wrong to "get the marriage job done" and move on. But I was wrong to let my hurt turn to anger, and exacerbate the problem. I should have modified my approach so I wouldn't have "sinned in my anger."

First, I should have expressed my hurt more assertively. I should have gone back to Bill again and again, using the conflict resolution techniques described in chapter 8, and repeated to him how I felt. I gave up too easily on the positive forms of communication and slipped too quickly into destructive patterns that drove us farther apart.

Of course, it is easy to say in retrospect what I should have done. In reality, asserting myself was no small task because my self-esteem had been severely damaged by Bill's shift. I no longer trusted my own insights. I was unsure of my feelings and opinions. In addition to that, because Bill was in the ministry, asking him to spend more time and energy on me meant that he would have less to devote to

L "God's work." That was a pretty heavy demand for a young wife to make.

I realize now that I should have talked with trusted friends who could have given me an accurate perspective on what was happening in our marriage. I needed objective outsiders who could affirm my position and give me the confidence to speak up, and also remind me of the dangers of holding back and allowing my hurt to turn to anger.

My next step, if communicating more assertively didn't help, should have been to suggest that Bill and I meet together with another couple. If Bill couldn't hear what I was saying, or if I was letting anger sabotage the process, perhaps our third-party friends could have moderated the communication process and facilitated understanding.

If that option didn't help, I should have suggested marriage counseling. If Bill refused to go, I should have gone to a counselor myself. I should have talked with someone who could have helped me process the hurt before it poisoned our relationship, and could have helped me formulate a workable plan of action or, as a last resort, an ultimatum.

An ultimatum? That's right. An ultimatum that would have caught Bill's attention. That would have forced action. That would have said, "I love you, but I can't take this anymore."

A short period of separation would have been one possible ultimatum. We have often wondered what effect a separation early in our marriage, monitored by a wise Christian counselor, would have had on the course of our relationship. It would have been traumatic, indeed, but it may well have broken a hurtful pattern that plagued us for years, minimized the damage done to our relationship, and significantly shortened the period of healing.

Seldom is one spouse responsible for ending the story of a romance. While one may be responsible for turning the page, the other's reaction may be what finally closes the book. To rewrite the story, both need to admit their sin, seek forgiveness, and adopt a new plan for the future.

THE PLACE TO START

What about you? Have you shifted gears and wounded your spouse? Have you become too preoccupied with competing demands? Have you allowed fatigue or financial problems or kids to drain the romance out of your marriage? Have you allowed the feelings to fade? Have you given up? Have you let hurt turn to anger? Have you concluded that you married the wrong person? Are you weary of the work of marriage? Do you lack the motivation to try again?

Maybe you need a private encounter with God. Maybe you need to take the blinders off and look at what Scripture says about marriage. Maybe you need to get down on your knees and commit yourself to becoming a wholehearted marriage partner. Maybe you need to say, "Forget what everybody else does. Forget what I've done in the past. Lord, out of gratitude for what You have done for me I want to obey You in every area of my life, including my marriage. I am going to begin treasuring my spouse. I am going to begin respecting my spouse. I am going to bring the romance back to my marriage."

If you are feeling overwhelmed by the challenge, please don't lose hope. God can help you rekindle your marriage. He offers you His motivation, His wisdom, His power, His encouragement, and His supernatural intervention. Ephesians 3:20 tells us that God "is able to do immeasurably more than all we ask or imagine."

But it's our move. We have to ask Him. We have to commit ourselves to obedience. Then God can bring the surprises. Not overnight. Not without work and pain and honest communication. But when His supernatural intervention comes to bear on our efforts, romance can be rekindled.

In the next chapter we want to look beyond the motivation to some of the practical mechanics of rebuilding romance.

Ten

Fanning the Flames of Marriage

L   It was a Wednesday in May, 1989. At 10 P.M., following our midweek church service, we loaded our luggage into our car and began a nighttime journey to a destination I did not know. It was our fifteenth wedding anniversary and Bill had made all the arrangements, including a baby-sitter for the kids. All I had to do was pack according to his careful instructions.

After two hours on the road we stopped at an all-night restaurant and had dessert. It was a truckstop that had marked the halfway point when we used to drive from Kalamazoo to Chicago during our dating years. Sometimes we made the trip to buy produce at Chicago's Water Street Market for Bill's dad. Other times Bill drove me back to college or picked me up for a weekend break. Sitting there eating hot apple pie, we reminisced about those years. We talked about how much we had enjoyed those drives. About the nonstop talk that had filled the eight-hour round trips. And about how we had hated seeing the Kalamazoo exit on the way back because it signaled our return to real life and our respective homes. By the time we resumed our journey, we felt like those dating kids again. Only this time we didn't have to meet a midnight curfew.

When we took the I-96 cutoff I guessed where we were headed, and I was right. Within an hour we were walking on the South Haven beach where we had walked on our first official date in 1969. There was the same concrete breaker upon which we had sat. The same lighthouse under which we had talked. The same moon whose beauty we had admired.

L   It was 3 A.M. We sat on the beach, digging our toes into the sand, watching the moonlit waves shimmy up the sodden bank. With each wave came a memory that crashed into our consciousness. A memory of a slammed door and a canceled courtship. Of making up, and of a carnival wedding. A memory of joy surrounding a baby's birth, and of tears shed in a cracker-box home. Of ministry moments that boggled our minds, and of a heartrending ride in a blue Suburban. Memories of a perfect vacation, of criticism and judgment, of celebrating uniqueness. Memories of feelings smothered by pain, and of a rekindled romance.

We were seventeen when we first sat together on that Lake Michigan beach—and naive. We foresaw only sunny days. By thirty-seven our naivete had been battered and finally destroyed by rainstorms and lightning and gale-force winds. But while our naivete had not survived, we had. We had come face to face with reality and we had stared it down. We had persevered and worked hard and won. And we sat on that beach stronger and more mature and more tolerant and more in love than ever.

Can a battered romance be rebuilt? Can the smoldering embers of dying feelings be refueled? We think they can be. We think that the love that drew a couple together in courtship can be recaptured and sustained, in spite of disappointments and setbacks and stormy weather. In this chapter we want to give some practical suggestions for doing just that.

TALK, TALK, TALK

Feelings grow best out of conversation, so that is where we want to start. Couples must devote themselves to talking—about anything, everything, important things, mundane things, pleasant things, disturbing things. Romance begins with knowledge of one another, and the key to knowledge is open, honest, consistent communication.

Our teenage daughter has a new boyfriend. Recently she spent a Saturday afternoon with him. They ran a few errands, then sat on a picnic table in a forest preserve and talked. "You talked?" we asked. "All afternoon? About what?"

"You know. About everything. About school and church

and our friends. About what we like and don't like. About what we're going to do this summer. About our goals. About college. About what makes us mad or happy. About you guys! It was wonderful."

Do you remember when there weren't enough hours in the day to contain your conversations? Do you remember how close you felt? How tuned in you were to each other?

Is it any wonder we lose the warmth in our relationships when we only talk on the run, when we leave each other memos on the kitchen table and messages on the answering machine? Too often spouses don't feel for one another anymore because they don't know one another anymore. They don't know each other's fears or dreams or goals or disappointments or plans. They don't know what goes on during each other's day. They aren't aware of the joys, the stresses, the responsibilities, the successes that fill their spouse's world.

Husbands and wives ought to find comfort in one another's presence. Their marriage should be a place of refuge. There ought to be an underlying sense that "it's you and me against the world." But it will never be that way unless spouses make time for in-depth communication on a regular basis. That is why a weekly date outside the home is so important. And why we need to take advantage of every opportunity to "catch up" on what is going on with our spouses. An after-dinner conversation while the kids clear the table, or an evening walk around the block, or even an afternoon telephone call to find out what the doctor said or how things went at the meeting can keep spouses informed and build on the sense of unity and caring established during more lengthy and significant conversations.

If the romance in your marriage has received a near-deadly blow, your conversations will undoubtedly have to begin by focusing on hidden hostilities. If you are like us, you are probably tempted to bypass this and move to more pleasant conversations. "The past is past," you say. "Let's forget it and move into the future." But that won't work. Underground hurts will undermine even your most earnest attempts to rebuild romance, and you will end up more frustrated than when you started.

"I know you didn't intend to hurt me, but you did. I felt

put down and rejected every time you said you were too busy to spend time with me." With those words, a friend of ours hoped to release once and for all the anger she felt toward her previously overscheduled husband. Because her husband was sincerely apologetic and committed to reopening the book on romance, she assumed she was free to focus on the future. But a short time later, she was again bursting with anger. "Do you realize what it was like to feel like the last item on your priority list? Do you realize how awful that was?"

That woman learned something very important about hidden hostilities: It is unrealistic to expect negative emotions that have built up over a number of years to dissipate in one conversation. People who have been deeply hurt need to give themselves the freedom to constructively express their hurt over and over again, if necessary. Those who caused the pain need to listen patiently, understanding that while working through past hurts can be painful and sometimes seem counterproductive, it is *essential* to rebuilding romance.

What complicates the process is that usually both spouses have caused hurt and received it. Sometimes a counselor can help sort through the confusion and assist spouses in asserting their own pain, while at the same time being sensitive to the other's pain. Again, it is tempting to jump over this step. But taking a responsible approach to past hurts, even if that means devoting six months or a year to counseling, will make the difference between smoldering embers and a roaring bonfire.

After you face up to past hurts and work through them, you can protect your new sense of unity and warmth by dealing with new conflicts as they arise. Planning frequent peace talks will clear the air and keep hurts from going underground again. Nothing destroys romance like an edge of anger. As the old adage says, it's no fun to hug a porcupine.

COURT CREATIVELY

After you get rid of hidden hostilities and learn what it means to talk again, you can begin to court creatively. Most couples put the wedding gifts away and their courting days behind them. But if you want to rebuild romance you need to court again.

Fortunately, courting is like riding a bike; you may get a little rusty, but you never forget how. So take a few minutes over lunch and write a simple note to your spouse. "I was just thinking about you and wanted to tell you I love you." "If I had it to do over again, I'd marry you in a minute. I'm excited about what the future will bring." Then put it in the mail. Imagine how your spouse will feel, expecting a list of chores you want done, and finding a love note instead.

Or you might consider calling your spouse during the day for no reason. "Hi. How are you? I was just wondering how your day was going." It means so much to a husband or wife to know that their spouse was thinking about them—and took the time to say it.

L   I know how busy Bill is when he is at the office, and he knows how hectic my day can be. So taking a few minutes to call and "check in" says something to both of us. It tells me that Bill cares more about me than the papers stacked on his desk and the calls he has to return. It tells him that the article I'm working on or the tasks that fill my day are not as important to me as he is.

Nonsexual touching is another important part of courting. If your first response to that sentence is that it is nonsense, it is no wonder the romance has drained out of your marriage. As important as sexual touch is—and we will talk about it later—warm, loving, nonsexual touch is every bit as essential to a romance-filled marriage.

Too many spouses do little more than give each other an obligatory kiss when they part ways in the morning and then repeat the routine when they greet one another at night. Their lips touch, but they barely even know it. It has become an involuntary response. Adding a little variety to touching can take it out of the autopilot realm and put the feeling back in it. When you take an after-dinner walk, reach down and grab your spouse's hand—and think about what you are doing. Let your clasped hands symbolize the lifetime commitment you have made to one another. While your spouse reads the paper, bend down and gently rub his or her neck; think of it as a comforting act of tenderness, as a way to ease the stress of a busy day. While you watch the nighttime news, put your arm around your spouse and say with that gesture, "I'm so glad we had another day to share together." An obligatory kiss is barely noticed. But touch that is backed by feeling is a match that can reignite a dying flame.

Flowers still spell romance. But don't just buy the daily special. Think back to your dating days. Did your spouse have a favorite flower? Was there a special occasion marked by a red rose? Do you recall a romantic evening complete with a beautiful corsage? Get creative. On your way to dinner, present your wife with a purple orchid like the one she wore to the prom. Buy a bouquet of sweetheart roses in honor of the flowers she carried on your wedding day.

If flowers never earned a place in your memory bank, don't despair. Ask your wife what kind she likes. Chances are she won't remember—it's been so long since it mattered—but give her time. Once the shock wears off and her senses return, she will describe the perfect bouquet. Ordering precisely what she describes will tell her that her preferences, her desires, her tastes matter to you. It will say, "I still treasure you."

Dating is another important part of courting. Watching our daughter prepare for a date is like watching the planning of a national event. First come the numerous phone calls to decide when to schedule the event. Then another slew of calls to discuss where to go for the event. Finally, there is a full-scale fashion show to determine what to wear to the event. Sadly, such enthusiasm wanes over the years. For many married couples, going out on a date is barely an event at all. They give it little thought or discussion ahead of time and squeeze it between "more important" commitments, go wherever the car takes them, and never consider dressing up "just for each other." No wonder their evenings out add little spark to their relationship.

We have friends who always discuss their Friday night date during dinner on the previous Monday. They look through the entertainment section of the Sunday newspaper, consider various options, then decide together what they want to do. Then they have all week to anticipate their plans and remind each other in notes or calls that "We're going to have a great time on Friday night," or "It's been a long week, but we'll be able to celebrate soon." They each make the evening more special by wearing clothes the other particularly likes. "I love it," says the wife, "when my husband walks out of the bedroom looking great in something he knows I like. It makes me feel like it's a real 'date,' the kind we enjoyed when we first met and were trying to catch each other's eye. It also tells me that my husband still thinks I'm worth 'looking good for.' That means a lot to me!"

Another aspect of courting creatively is serving one another. During high school a young man carries his girlfriend's books and she makes him chocolate chip cookies. In college he hauls her suitcases and she types his term paper. During engagement he fixes her car and she does his laundry. (Or vice versa.) But six months after the wedding, they retire their servant's uniforms. Suddenly it's every man for himself; every woman for herself. They hide the uniforms in the back of the hallway closet, and with them the warm feelings that service engenders. If a husband and wife want to heat up those feelings again, they need to squeeze themselves back into those uniforms, blow the dust off the shoulders, and get back to serving. Discovering and joyfully offering small acts of service that bring special delight to a spouse is a great way to change the tone of a relationship.

B   After fifteen years of driving high-mileage, boat-sized, family vehicles, Lynne made the switch to a new, downsized, red Toyota that she loves. It represents a rite of passage for her, a delightful freedom from hauling cribs and car seats and bicycles and basketball teams. One way I have found to serve her is to make sure her little car is never less than sparkling. I blow the budget on Turtle Wax and Armor All, but it's worth it to see the smile on her face when she slides behind the wheel of an immaculate car.

In spite of the influence of the women's movement, women still tend to end up doing more than their share of mundane, time-consuming, exhausting, thankless household tasks. One way for husbands to get beyond cheap talk is to cheerfully and voluntarily assume more of these responsibilities. During the early years of our marriage I flagrantly violated this principle. Since then I have learned that planning special activities for the kids, or doing the

B dishes, or putting away the groceries, or vacuuming the
{ living room, or making travel arrangements, or stopping at
the dry cleaners are essential though neglected parts of
romance.

Creative courting also includes inspiring our spouses. Do
you remember how often you used to cheer each other on when
you were dating? "You have so much potential!" "You're going
to be a great lawyer someday." "You can succeed at whatever
you choose." "You belong on the stage; you played that role
perfectly." "I'll stand by you no matter what." "I can't wait to
see you soar." "That was great how you caught that line drive
this afternoon." "You have tremendous gifts and abilities." "I'm
so proud of you." But now that you've settled into life's
routines, do you even pay attention to what your spouse is
doing? Do you comment on accomplishments or encourage
after failures? Are you the biggest cheerleader your spouse has?

When we started our church we took a door-to-door
survey of our community. We asked people who didn't regularly
attend church what there was about church that drove them
away. The most common complaint was that church services
were dull, repetitive, routine, and predictable. Unfortunately,
that same complaint can be made of many marriages. That is
why we talk about courting creatively. While boredom puts
both church members and spouses to sleep, creativity has a
powerful way of jarring people awake and exciting their
emotions. Creativity tells a spouse that rebuilding romance is
important to you. It is worthy of your time, your thought, your
energy. It is a priority. After years of neglect, that is often the
message a spouse most needs to hear. It is the jump-start that
can get damaged feelings working again.

LANGUAGE OF LOVE

Although we offered a few specific suggestions about
courting creatively, only you can determine the best way to
court your spouse. Why? Because every husband and every wife
is different and has different ways of giving and receiving love.
In order to court your spouse meaningfully, you need to
determine which is his or her preferred *language of love*.

For some people touch is the primary language of love.

Their spouse can say "I love you" twenty times a day and prove it through countless actions of kindness, but without an embrace or a kiss or a squeeze they won't *feel* loved.

Other people need to hear verbal expressions of love. They need to hear in concrete terms why their spouse loves them. "I'm glad I married you because . . ." assures them that their spouse recognizes and appreciates their individuality.

Service is what makes some people feel most loved. They respond best to affection that is revealed in practical terms: cooking a meal, mowing the lawn, repairing a faucet, running an errand, helping with a distasteful chore. These people see acts of service as indicative of what is in their spouse's heart.

Gifts make other people feel loved—not because of the cost involved, but because of the personal attention and thought that goes into them. These people enjoy—even need—tangible reminders of their spouse's love.

Some people feel loved when their spouse offers them opportunities for pleasure or self-improvement. They appreciate a spouse who says, "I heard of a seminar I think you would enjoy. Why don't you take it?" That convinces them that their spouse cares about the things that are important to them.

Spending time together makes other people feel loved. They don't care particularly what they and their spouses do, as long as they are together. Having their husband or wife commit uninterrupted blocks of time to them assures them they are top priority.

Do you know which language of love is important to your spouse?

B For years I assumed that the best way to convince Lynne that I loved her was to remind her repeatedly why I had married her. "I really appreciate your spirituality," I'd tell her, "and your intelligence and your conscientiousness. I respect your character, and I think you'll make a great mother someday." I was sure that would make her feel loved.

But it didn't. She appreciated it, but it wasn't enough to convince her of my love. She needed to receive love through the language of touch; she needed lots of physical affection. She also needed my time. She needed me to take

B the initiative in setting aside quiet hours on a regular basis when we could be together. For years, I gave her neither.

Why did I assume that verbal expressions of love would do the job? Because that was the love language I preferred. It made me feel great when Lynne told me she was proud of something I had done or that she loved a certain aspect of my character or personality. I didn't need her to hug me or squeeze my hand or spend large blocks of time with me, as much as I needed her to build me up with her words. I needed to know she loved and respected the unique qualities that made me *me*. So I assumed that was all she needed.

Making assumptions about the language of love our spouse prefers often leads to disappointment, and sometimes even to misunderstanding.

L Another way Bill showed love to me was by providing me with opportunities—more than I could possibly take advantage of. He was always saying, "You should take that writing assignment. You would do a superb job." Or, "That is a great speaking opportunity. You would really minister to those women." Or, "You should join me on this trip. You would have fun and meet lots of interesting people." Or, "Why don't you sign up for a wilderness survival weekend? You would learn so much."

On one hand, I appreciated the confidence he seemed to have in my abilities. On the other hand, it seemed that he wasn't satisfied with me the way I was. He was always pushing me to do more, accomplish more, relate more, learn more. And taking advantage of even a fraction of the opportunities he threw my way filled my time to overflowing and created a high level of stress.

When I finally told him how I felt, he was shocked. "I get a kick out of providing opportunities for the people I love," he said. "I wasn't trying to 'push' you."

Bill is a wonderful leader, friend, and father because he delights in opening doors of opportunity for those around him. That's his most comfortable and natural way of expressing love. When I came to understand that, I began

L to appreciate the opportunities he provided and began to
{ feel loved instead of "pushed." I was free to respond to
{ those that interested me and say "No thanks" to the rest.

Husbands and wives need to pinpoint their own and their spouse's preferred languages of love, and then negotiate a way to make sure they both receive love in the language they can understand. That often requires flexibility, sensitivity, and a willingness to grow in areas where we may be weak.

L   As mentioned earlier, Bill hears love best when it's
{ expressed in verbal terms. He needs me to tell him that I
{ love him—and tell him why in creative, meaningful,
{ specific terms. Unfortunately, verbal expression is not my
{ strong suit. I have had to remind myself daily that Bill
{ needs my words, just as he has had to remind himself daily
{ that I need physical affection. And when either of us gets
{ careless or forgetful, the other has to put pride aside and be
{ vulnerable enough to say, "I'm not feeling very loved.
{ Would you please say it again in terms I can understand."

FOCUS ON THE FUN SIDE

If you want to rekindle romance, you should commit yourself to meaningful conversation, court creatively, learn one another's language of love, and now, start to have some fun again.

It may help to think back to your dating years and try to recapture some of the fun moments you shared then. Brush up on your tennis skills. Go to an afternoon baseball game. Spend a Saturday at the beach. Set up a volleyball net in the backyard. Go to a concert. Plan a picnic. Ride bikes through the country. Walk through an art gallery. Go to a silly movie. Roast marshmallows over a bonfire.

It is so easy for life to get too serious. Couples talk about money and kids, about jobs and responsibilities, about fears and old age. And they forget what it means to laugh and to play and to feel like kids again.

Even the best marriages take a tremendous amount of work. If there is no fun to balance out the work, even the most earnest spouses begin to lose motivation and energy. And the more challenging a marriage is, the more important fun is. We have learned that mutually enjoyable, fun experiences can help heal tender wounds and become a bridge across frustrating differences.

We enjoy attending cultural events together, reading the same books and comparing insights, and spending time with mutual friends. But our most enjoyable activities tend to center around sports. We both love sailing and water skiing, hiking and snow skiing, and running and working out together. Because of our differences, we were delighted to discover these common interests and deliberately plan many marital and family occasions around these mutual activities. If we want to plan a weekend getaway that is a "sure thing" we'll go where there are plenty of walking trails or a lake with rental sailboats. We have learned that a healthy shot of fun can carry us through a lot of hard work, so we make no apology for scheduling fun as often as we can.

Several years ago we talked with a Christian man who had committed adultery. Putting a loving hand on our shoulders, he begged us to commit ourselves to having fun in our marriage. "I have always loved my wife," he said. "But our relationship became businesslike. We poured our energy into our jobs, raising our children, helping in the community, and serving together in our church, but we didn't take time to have fun together. So, when someone came along and offered me laughter and lightheartedness, a respite from all the work and responsibility, I was a sitting duck. I fell for the promise of a little fun. How I wish my wife and I had taken the time to play."

How is the fun factor in your marriage? If it needs a boost, begin to experiment. Schedule a variety of activities and see which ones you like. Take a class together and see if you can discover a new interest. Ask other couples for ideas. Look in the entertainment section of your local newspaper. Be open-minded. Be bold. Try new things. Fun and laughter have a wonderful way of breaking down inhibitions, generating warmth, and leading to . . .

EVEN MORE FUN

If you have been wondering when we were going to get around to talking about sex, you need wonder no longer. We have waited till the end of the chapter to discuss it because we have learned that mutually satisfying sex starts with communication, creative courting, meaningful expressions of love, and shared fun. The actual act of sex is the culmination of a series of encounters that set the tone and create the desire for total, loving, physical intimacy.

We believe sex should be the ultimate fun activity a couple shares. Unfortunately, for many couples, including us during the early years of our marriage, sex provides more frustration than fun. A small percentage of couples suffer from true sexual dysfunctions of either physical or psychological origins. We encourage them to consult a doctor or a counselor. Applying simplistic answers to their complex problems would only increase their frustration.

Even aside from sexual dysfunctions, human sexuality is very complex and affected by a myriad of personal and relational factors. Obviously we cannot, in a few short pages, look in depth at such a broad subject. We have found, however, that many couples in the process of rebuilding romance can benefit from a slight shift in attitude or from a few fresh ideas regarding sexual experience. That's what we needed.

FUN FOR WHOM?

Like many young married couples, we read our share of books about sex. We easily dismissed those authors who viewed sexual intercourse solely as a means of procreation, and appreciated authors who acknowledged that God had designed human sexuality, in part at least, for married people's pleasure. Such authors described sexual pleasure as a priceless gift spouses can give to one another—a gift, in fact, that they *must* give to one another.

The notion of sex as something important we must give to our spouses is biblical. First Corinthians 7 teaches clearly that spouses must fulfill their "marital duty" to one another, and must not "deprive each other." According to this passage, a wife does not have authority over her own body; her husband does. Similarly, she has authority over his. These verses are not-so-subtle reminders that we each owe our spouse a satisfying sexual relationship. We are, after all, our spouse's only sexual option.

The commitment to marital fidelity, which every sincere Christian couple must make, means that if we don't find sexual fulfillment in our marriage, we don't find it. It is as simple, and sometimes as tragic, as that. Each of us must take our sexual responsibility seriously, and lovingly and enthusiastically do everything in our power to meet and fulfill our spouse's sexual needs and desires.

Having said all that, we want to briefly mention the flip side of healthy sex. We believe that putting too much emphasis on sex as something one does for his or her spouse can have a negative effect on some people's attitudes. For these people sex becomes one more obligation, one more task they need to perform to be a "good wife" or a "good husband." They forget that sex is something they should enjoy *for themselves*.

Some people don't enjoy sex because they don't enjoy their own sexuality. Some husbands and wives, in fact, don't even view themselves as sexual beings. Sex is something they *do*, an out-of-character behavior they squeeze in at the end of a busy day, rather than a natural extension of an important dimension of who they are. These people would become more interested and interesting sexual partners if they would give themselves permission to enjoy their sexuality, view their sexuality as an important part of their identity, and take delight in excelling sexually. People who take a positive approach to their sexuality, and commit themselves to developing their sexual skills just as they develop their other gifts and skills, cultivate a sexual confidence that frees them to become active rather than passive participants in a sexual relationship. They become proactive sexually rather than merely reactive. And they bring tremendous pleasure to their spouses.

L   Diapers. Dinner. Dishes. Sex. They were all part of the same routine, all part of my responsibility as a wife and mother. And all about equally enjoyable.

But somewhere along the way I began to see sex differently. I began to view it as a diversion, an escape, a chance to crawl out from under routine responsibilities and mundane chores. A chance to put on a new hat, to be somebody different. A chance to have some fun right in my own home, without having to buy a ticket or pay a baby-

L sitter. I began to view it as a break that I deserved, a
romantic reward.

When I began to view sex as something fun I could do
for myself, when I quit focusing my attention solely on
what would make Bill happy and started thinking about
what would please me as well, I became a much more
exciting sexual partner. I no longer had to worry about
pleasing Bill. I *was* pleasing him. He would say, in fact, that
my new attitude marked a dramatically positive turning
point in our sexual relationship. When a wife experiences
maximum pleasure herself, that multiplies her husband's
pleasure.

We're not talking about selfish sex. We assume that
husbands and wives are committed to satisfying each other
sexually, and that they will be sensitive to one another's unique
needs and preferences and desires. What we're talking about is
authentic, fully engaged, mutually enjoyable, genuinely fun sex.

GETTING STARTED

Fun sex doesn't start in the bedroom. It starts in the
kitchen, during a private moment when a nonsexual touch slides
over into the realm of the blatantly sexual. It begins with a
playful suggestion of sexual intent, or a not-so-subtle sexual
innuendo, or a well-placed flirtatious remark.

B Over the years we have developed our own *physical love
language*. When I leave for the evening and Lynne
whispers, "If you make it home from your board meeting
on time tonight, I'll make it worth your while," I don't
have to wonder what she means. I know that's an open
invitation, and you can bet I get home on time. This may
explain the efficiency of our board meetings!

When I'm traveling, and I call home and Lynne says,
"You don't know what you're missing tonight," I know
that's her way of telling me I have an interested wife
waiting at home. And it seriously tempts me to hop a plane
for O'Hare.

Another way to encourage sexual enthusiasm is to actively

build one another's concept of desirability. Husbands and wives will be much more interested in sex if they feel like desirable sexual partners.

L   With the unavoidable media onslaught of strikingly beautiful, sexually stimulating, airbrushed female bodies, real live women need a heavy dose of sexual affirmation. We need to know that even though we don't have perfect bodies we have the power to excite and delight our husbands.

Bill constantly compliments me in specific, sexually oriented terms. He knows the physical characteristics I feel uncomfortable about, and sensitively reassures me about those. He also makes a big point of "talking up" my positive physical attributes. He goes out of his way to convince me that my physical liabilities are of the sort that make little difference to him, while my assets are of the sort that make his day.

My sexual confidence, and my ability to enjoy my sexuality, are strongly tied to Bill's enthusiastic, consistent, verbal affirmation of my sexual desirability. Many spouses wish their husbands or wives had greater sexual interest and confidence. They don't realize the power they have to instill that confidence through affirmation and compliments.

How spouses dress is another way they can heighten—or squelch—sexual desire. We know that for some people dress truly makes little difference. Most spouses admit, however, that what their husband or wife wears affects their sexual interest.

L   One beautiful spring day Bill confiscated my favorite, well-worn nightgown, ripped it into irregular squares, and used it as a rag to wash the car. He had previously suggested that I terminate my love affair with that gown, but I hadn't taken him seriously. Now I had no choice.

I retaliated by spending an afternoon in the designer pajama section of a department store looking for a replacement for Bill's favorite "loungewear"—a torn T-shirt and baggy sweats.

L   Seriously, we have had some very frank discussions about dress. I have tended to be an overly modest, safe dresser. Bill has tended to be an overly casual, careless dresser. He finally admitted that he would prefer a little more pizzazz (a subtle seductive flair, he calls it) in my dress, particularly at home. I finally admitted that I would prefer a little more style in his dress, at home *and* abroad.

Maybe you think this is an insignificant point. After all, how we dress is a purely temporal concern, a relatively trivial issue in the scheme of life. But temporal or not, we have found that it affects the sexual climate in our marriage. So we think it's something worth paying attention to.

Maintaining good health is another way to enhance sexual interest. The general sense of well-being and increased body consciousness that come from regular exercise enhance sexuality. Eating right and getting enough sleep are important, too. Everybody knows that exhaustion is one of the greatest sex-busters.

Other sure sex-busters are hostility and lack of creativity, which is why we started this chapter the way we did. Working through hidden hostilities and learning to court creatively are essential to enhancing sexual interest.

AGAIN—TALK, TALK, TALK

Each couple's physical relationship is unique. Some couples couldn't imagine a sexual encounter without music and candle-light. Others prefer silence and the cloak of darkness. For some people, exhaustion makes an evening rendezvous impractical; they prefer morning get-togethers. For others, even the thought of a morning sexual encounter is laughable. Preferred frequency of sex is also highly variable.

Instead of taking your cues from Hollywood or from other couples, why not develop your own sexual style. Experiment. Explore new avenues of sexual expression. And above all, communicate. Talk openly, vulnerably, specifically, and regularly about your sexual relationship. We have observed a direct correlation between a couple's level of sexual communication and their level of sexual fulfillment. Too many people expect their spouses to "just know" what they want sexually, then do a slow burn when their spouses don't come through.

A more constructive option is to openly discuss issues directly related to sexuality. You might suggest ways your spouse could help you feel more sexually desirable, and ask for ideas about how you could do the same in return. Another idea is to describe the kinds of circumstances, events, or conversations that are most likely to spark your sexual interest. You could also talk about guaranteed turnoffs, personal sex-busters, and past sexual disappointments. Or you could describe your best recent sexual memories, and explain what made those experiences so good. Sharing specific ideas about what you can each do, say, or wear to capture the other's sexual attention would also be helpful.

For some couples these questions are terribly threatening. Husbands and wives who have never talked openly about their sexual relationship often find it very hard to get started. Picking one question and discussing it after a day of lighthearted fun may be the best way for such couples to start. Eventually they can move into more in-depth discussions and even begin a little undercover research.

Sensitive, open communication is a hefty challenge, whether you are discussing a backlog of anger or a way to spice up a less-than-sizzling sexual relationship. But it always pays high dividends. So give it a try. Prop up the pillows on your bed, make yourself comfortable, and talk openly with your spouse about sex. You just might be glad you did.

We were.

Eleven

Living in Crisis Mode

B   It was a Saturday morning in December of 1989. I went to my office early to finish the sermon I had to give that evening at church. At five-thirty A.M. I was on page twelve of my message. By one-thirty P.M. I was on page eight. I was in big trouble.

To complicate matters, I had to do a wedding before five hundred people that afternoon, and I hadn't given one thought to what I was going to say to the young couple and their gathered family and friends. I thought about my unfinished message, about the wedding, and about the evening church service, and in a moment of total frustration, I laid my head down on my desk and cried.

Almost before the first teardrop hit the desk I reminded myself that falling apart was a ridiculous waste of time, and I quickly mopped myself up. But in that brief moment of "losing it" I had seen the truth: The wheels were coming off my carefully constructed wagon.

That fall our church had added another weekly service, which meant that I taught Wednesday, Thursday, and Saturday nights, and twice on Sunday morning. In between message preparation and actual teaching, I squeezed an increasing load of administrative duties and travel commitments. I had thought I was up to the challenge of an increased teaching schedule, and I had charged into the autumn months prepared to run the kingdom race as hard and fast as I'd ever run it before. But all of a sudden, it seemed I couldn't run at all.

I hobbled through the fall, hanging on till Christmas vacation. I left with my family for what was supposed to be a quiet family retreat. Through unforeseen events, we ended up instead in a hotel mob scene. It was the kind of place where you had to wait twenty minutes for an

B elevator, and when the elevator came it was so crowded
   you couldn't get in. That was the last straw. I was in a mild
   state of frenzy the entire week.

       When we got home I went alone to Wisconsin for three
   days to recuperate, think, and pray. "God, what's happening to me? I don't understand what's going on in my life,
   but I feel like I'm going under. Help me."

       I spent the following year putting the pieces of my life
   back together. By delegating certain ministry responsibilities I was able to continue working, but at a greatly
   reduced pace. The remainder of my time I devoted to
   personal healing and to some long-overdue reflection on a
   pattern of life that had finally driven me to the breaking
   point.

BEWARE OF ACHILLES' HEEL

It was just a small spot of weakness on the mythical
warrior's heel, but it led to his death in the Trojan War. Since
classical times we have borrowed from the Greek legend the
notion of a nagging vulnerability with the power to bring a
strong man—or woman—down. Everyone has an Achilles'
heel. The wise among us, who recognize their weaknesses and
carefully protect them from attack, stand firm; the unwise, who
leave their weaknesses exposed, are downed in the battle.

One problem with an Achilles' heel—whatever form it
takes—is that it follows us into marriage. In this chapter and the
next we want to expose our respective Achilles' heels because we
have discovered, in looking back over seventeen years of
marriage, that our individual weak spots have complicated our
relationship more than anything else we have discussed thus far.

L   Bill's Achilles' heel is his overdevotion to work and
    ministry, and in the latter months of 1989 it almost ruined
    him.

        It had nearly destroyed our relationship years before, but
    as we mentioned in a previous chapter, after five years of
    marriage Bill made some dramatic schedule changes. For
    the sake of our marriage and family life, he committed
    himself to maintaining our Thursday morning breakfast

L dates and to being home four nights a week. This
commitment to being home more meant he regularly
turned down requests to attend or speak at church
.meetings and at outside events. If his travel schedule
interfered with time set aside for family, he made up the
lost time as soon as possible: He scheduled a special outing
with the kids or planned a make-up date with me. He also
took an annual summer break, dedicated both to personal
study and family fun. And he put time and creativity into
planning family getaways throughout the year. He took
our marriage and family life very, very seriously. Even
when his work responsibilities increased he maintained his
commitment to being home.

As the years passed, however, I began to see a change in
Bill. More and more I sensed that he was home in body
only. His mind was somewhere else, preoccupied with
concerns that had nothing to do with home. Whereas in
the past he had been an active contributor to our family
life, he seemed now to have little to give. He wasn't
unpleasant or unkind, but he was always exhausted. Home
was where he came to crash. The kids and I had to tiptoe
through the evening so as not to disturb him.

"Shh, Daddy's resting."

"No, you can't disturb him now. He needs to recuperate."

"Maybe you can talk to him tomorrow."

He was home; he hadn't violated his commitment. But
we certainly weren't enjoying his presence. He poured
nearly all his energy into his work, and we got an empty,
cracked shell we had to patch together and send back to the
office.

Bill's Achilles' heel led him into a style of life so fast-
paced it drained every ounce of emotional energy out of
him and undermined our most earnest attempts to build a
mutually satisfying marriage. He was living in what we call
"crisis mode."

KEEPING IT PEGGED IN THE RED

Crisis mode living is when you spend every waking
moment of every day trying to figure out how to keep all your

balls in the air and all your plates spinning. In crisis mode you keep running faster and faster, from project to project, deadline to deadline, quota to quota, meeting to meeting, sermon to sermon. Your RPMs keep creeping higher and higher until you hit the red line.

Most active people have to spend a certain amount of time in crisis mode. Life just turns out that way. You're an accountant during tax season. You repair air conditioners and it's August in Phoenix. You're cramming to take the bar exam. Your kids are breaking out with chicken pox. You have two weeks to meet a sales quota.

The problem arises when you spend too much time in crisis mode. That's when crisis mode goes from being a season of life to becoming a way of life. When that happens—when you keep the needle pegged in the red week after week, month after month—you start doing the only thing you can do. You economize. You shortchange your investment of energy in certain areas of your life so you can invest it in other areas— usually in the performance-oriented areas to which your self-esteem is tied. Nothing matters but keeping those all-important balls in the air and those ultimately significant plates spinning, so you use all your energy accomplishing those feats. In every other area of life, you become a miser; you hoard your energy, you engage minimally, you touch superficially, you slide along the surface, you *skim*.

First, you skim relationally. Your bond with your spouse that used to be strong and intimate becomes increasingly weak and distant. You hope he or she doesn't have a serious need because you don't have energy to deal with it. You hydroplane over conflicts. You put Band-Aids on serious problems. You resort to quick fixes, and pretend things really aren't so bad.

You also skim with your kids. You don't keep track of them too well anymore. You no longer know what is going on in their lives. Little signs of trouble grab your attention, but you push them out of your mind. Warning flags wave, but you turn your head. You don't have the energy to face them—not now, anyway. Maybe tomorrow. Or maybe they will just go away.

Your friendships that used to be so deep and accountable are now characterized by shallowness. Your casual friendships don't even exist anymore. Pretty soon, nobody has access to you because you are so busy juggling and spinning.

You also skim in your relationship with God. You reduce your prayers to cries of desperation. You reduce worship to thanking God for helping you survive the madness of another week. You run too fast for reflection or meditation, for introspection or confession. You begin rationalizing little sins, and then bigger ones. Before you know it, you have journeyed far from spiritual innocence.

Then you start skimming emotionally. You find that your anger is flaring up more than it used to, but you don't take time to figure out why. You no longer pay attention to feelings like hurt or sadness or guilt. You become a mechanical soldier: You just keep marching, doing what is necessary, and stuffing your feelings deeper and deeper inside. If you knew that those stuffed feelings were huddling together and planning an emotional insurrection that would one day scare the daylights out of you, you might pay attention to them. But you don't know that. Besides, you don't have the energy to go peeking under stones and trudging through the sticky muck of your emotional life. You don't have time to look inside.

CHECK *ALL* THE GAUGES

Even if you have time to consider your emotional condition, chances are you won't. The Christian community has a pretty good track record for ignoring the emotional side of life. When it comes to reading the gauges on the dashboard of their psyche, most Christians look at only one gauge: the spiritual one. They assume that if they are sincerely walking with Christ, if they are praying and receiving sound teaching, if they are worshiping publicly and privately, then everything is okay.

A few Christians go a step further and check out the physical gauge. They believe, as we do, that part of Christian obedience, part of making ourselves fully available for God's use, is to take care of their bodies. So they eat birdseed and tree bark, and lift weights and do aerobic exercises. They are convinced that if they keep the spiritual and physical gauges in order they will be able to work hard, stand firm, and win the battles until the day they die.

But as crucial as those gauges are, there is a third gauge, the emotional gauge, and neglecting to pay attention to it has been the downfall of many spiritually strong and physically healthy people.

We have observed that nearly everyone faces at least one massive, energy-draining reality. It may be a financial pressure or a health concern or a rebellious teenager. It could be a handicapped child or a personality conflict with a friend or neighbor. For some people it's a demanding boss or a pending lawsuit. Others get bogged down by the ongoing trauma of a difficult marriage, or the daily drain of a high-stress job. Sometimes it's just an unpleasant responsibility that can't be ignored. Whatever it is, it repeatedly drains one's emotional tanks.

In addition, people living in crisis mode usually face a long list of smaller energy-draining realities every day. So at the end of every twenty-four-hour period, their emotional gauges read empty, and they end up living their lives in a constant state of emotional depletion.

A SHRINKING HEART

The emotional depletion that results from living in crisis mode eventually produces a *shrinking heart*. This is a heart that does not worship as authentically as it once did, or love God as passionately as it used to. It is a heart that is no longer sensitive to the needs of others, a heart that has lost the fire of compassion.

While the hearts of healthy Christians keep enlarging to encompass more of the heart of Christ, the hearts of Christians in crisis mode become shriveled and weak. A man from our church said, "You're right about the crisis mode. I have a bigger staff, a bigger budget, a bigger building, a bigger house, a bigger bank account, and a bigger belt line than I had five years ago. And all I have to show for it is a hollow cavern where my heart used to be."

B   I know exactly what that man meant. I learned about it
)   firsthand during the summer following the emotional crash
     described at the beginning of this chapter. Though I had

B begun to make some necessary life changes, I was still depleted emotionally when Lynne and the kids and I arrived in Michigan for our annual summer break.

The day after we arrived I talked with a friend in a local store. Just as we ended our conversation and I headed for the exit door, I noticed a Vietnam veteran in a motorized wheelchair who I had seen around town the previous summer. He was leaving the store too, and arrived at the exit shortly ahead of me. While I waited impatiently for him to jockey his wheelchair through the narrow doorway, an unsettling awareness began churning inside me.

I sensed the Holy Spirit saying, "Take a look inside you right now, Bill. Isn't it true that you are more upset about the inconvenience of waiting thirty seconds to get out this door than about the broken dreams this man carries in his motorized wheelchair? Isn't it true that your trivial inconvenience causes you more heartache than this man's tragedy?"

I walked to my car thinking, *What's wrong with me? I used to love people. I used to have compassion. I used to be moved by the lost, the needy, the hurting. Now all I care about is my convenience: "Don't bother me, pal. Get out of my way." I ought to be arrested!*

I spent the next four or five weeks replenishing myself emotionally. I separated myself from the pressures of ministry. I read for pleasure. I did fun, relaxing activities with my family. I enjoyed lighthearted conversations with close friends. I spent time alone.

One afternoon I was out running, and I saw that same Vietnam vet coming down the other side of the street in his wheelchair. When he was directly across the street from me I turned to look at him. Our eyes met, and it was like God gave me X-ray vision. I felt as if I were peering deep into his soul, and I began to cry over the heartbreak of his life. He was just about my age, and had probably dreamed the same dreams and held the same aspirations that I had dreamed and held in my youth. But somewhere in a hostile jungle he had stepped on a land mine, and his whole life had come crashing in on him.

B He turned and wheeled up a concrete ramp into a tiny clapboard cottage, and I was saddened to see him disappear. I wanted to reach out to him, talk to him, show him that I cared. I was filled with a swell of emotion.

While I continued my run, I thought about what had happened. I sensed the Holy Spirit saying, "You're on your way back, Bill. Your emotional tanks are filling, and you're starting to feel again. You're beginning to have compassion again."

SEDUCED BY SIN

While emotional depletion is often ignored, the havoc it plays in our lives cannot be ignored. In addition to draining the compassion out of our hearts, emotional depletion also leaves us vulnerable to sin. People who are emotionally exhausted, or whose emotions have been neglected, begin to cry out on a psychological level for comfort, for release, for escape, for something that will make them feel good or satiate their senses. They begin to crave quick hits of pleasure. They are lured by temptations that had never tempted them before. Activities they had never considered suddenly become live options.

B I couldn't figure out what was going on in me during the months before my summer break. I kept recalling a song recorded by Burt Reynolds: "Let's Do Something Cheap and Superficial." The tantalizing words kept playing over and over in my mind.

I didn't fall to that which tempted me, but I talked to others who had. I told them about my emotional depletion, and about my nagging desire to escape in ways I had never considered before. Over and over I heard the same response.

"That's how I felt before I fell to sin."

"That's what led to my demise."

"That's where I went wrong."

In the previous chapter we mentioned that a Christian man who had committed adultery challenged us to make fun a priority in our marriage. He also told us to keep careful watch over our emotional gauges. "Don't let the tanks run low," he warned. "When you get emotionally drained, you begin to crave a quick fix. And too often quick fixes present themselves in the form of illicit relationships. There's something about a clandestine meeting or a secret conversation that provides the kind of fast-acting high an emotionally depleted person craves. But it's a high that guarantees a bad trip."

OPT FOR A SLOW CHARGE

If a fast-acting high isn't the answer to emotional depletion, what is? A trickle charge.

If you were to go out in your garage and turn on every accessory in your car, you could probably drain the battery in about five minutes. To recharge it, you would have two choices. First, there is the quick charge. This is a fast-acting method that gets cars running in record time, but if used frequently it burns out the plates in the battery. Second, there is the method all responsible mechanics suggest: the trickle charge. With this approach, it takes six to eight hours to get a battery recharged to full strength, but it doesn't burn out the plates. It replaces the lost energy *and* preserves the life of the battery.

Drained emotional batteries need a trickle charge, too. A trickle charge involves determining what replenishes you emotionally and then incorporating that into your schedule. It also means spacing your emotionally draining responsibilities in such a way that in between them you can trickle charge back up to emotional fullness. In our culture that is no small challenge.

Today's modern technology makes it possible for men and women to carry tremendous amounts of responsibility and to make every minute count. A pastor can conduct planning meetings on his car phone on the way to the airport, write sermons on his lap-top computer on the plane, speak in five cities in two days, and fax up-to-the-minute memos to his church staff. And that story is repeated in every other profession.

We finish one emotionally draining activity and have fifteen minutes before the next one starts. We run to the microwave, slide in a plate of pasta, and after thirty seconds, complain that "this thing takes forever!" The speed of our lives makes it impossible to recharge.

In Jesus' day, it may well have been easier to live a balanced life. Imagine that after speaking to a crowd in Jerusalem, Jesus decides to walk the fifteen or so miles to Jericho with his twelve disciples. They walk for a couple hours, then stop to cool off under a fig tree. They tell a few jokes, eat a few grapes, then slowly move on. A while later they pause at a well and chat with other travelers watering their camels, then they enjoy a drink themselves before hitting the road again. Before they know it, it's dinner time, so they wander off the beaten path to gather wood for a fire. They quickly build a flaming pyramid of dry branches, but it takes some time for the coals to get hot. By the time dinner is done, it's dusk—no time to travel—so they settle in for the night, gathering round the roaring blaze to talk over the day.

We don't mean to minimize the rigors of first-century travel, but it's more than likely that something very healthy happened during those long hours of mundane activity. There was physical exercise, friendly conversation, long stretches of quiet for reflection and planning, and plenty of time for emotional reserves to trickle charge before the next draining demand.

B That healthy pattern was definitely not a part of my life. Crisis mode living never leaves time for a trickle charge. So my first step in building up my emotional reserves was to get out of crisis mode.

I realized that what had shoved me into crisis mode was too much teaching. I was spending almost every waking moment of every day thinking about, praying about, reading about, writing about, preparing for, or recuperating from giving messages. Even when I was meeting with my staff, or spending an evening with friends, or relating to Lynne and the kids, I was feeling the weight of message preparation, and I was preoccupied.

I prayed about the situation, and sensed that the answer was a team approach to teaching at our church, but most Christian leaders from whom I sought counsel said it wouldn't work. *You can't have more than one primary teacher*

B *in a given church. The congregation will be torn. It will split the church. There will be competition between teachers. Lines of authority will blur. The staff management structure will crumble. It is too radical. Too risky.*

But I knew that I needed to make a radical change. The size of my heart depended on it. The shape of my marriage depended on it. I had to take the risk.

In the fall of 1990 I divvied up a year's worth of weekend and midweek services between myself and three other teachers. Contrary to some people's fear, the change has been overwhelmingly positive for our church. And for me, it has proven to be exactly what I needed. I have been able to escape the madness of crisis mode living and enter a whole new way of life.

PLAYING GAMES

But getting out of crisis mode is only the beginning. Reorganizing our lives and establishing a more manageable schedule opens time for a trickle charge. But then we need to discover the specific activities that can provide the charge and replenish us emotionally. We need to incorporate into our schedules the forms of recreation that truly do "recreate" us.

B It didn't take me long to figure out what I had to do. In fact, when I looked back over the years I could see clearly why I had ended up emotionally exhausted. When I first went into ministry I had all kinds of hobbies and recreational thrills and chills. Athletics were a big part of my life—I loved car and motorcycle racing, snow skiing, flying, water skiing, football, softball, basketball—and they were effective energizers and stress reducers. My ministry demands were also much lighter then, so I had relatively low responsibility and a lot of fun and recreation.

Between 1973 and 1989, however, my responsibilities skyrocketed, while my rest and recreational levels plummeted: I no longer had time for playing games. So at thirty-eight years old, I ended up with a heavy mantle of ministry pressure draped across my shoulders, and almost no recreational releases.

B   After my crash, I realized I had to slow down enough to reintegrate recreational athletics into my life. During the summer of 1990 I enrolled in a professional race driving school to address my "need for speed." I also experienced the adrenaline rush of learning how to barefoot ski—and taught Lynne how, too. In the fall I joined a Park District football league, and I even played a little golf. It was like hooking myself up to an IV dripping undiluted emotional energy. Each week I felt healthier than I had the week before.

Along the way, I found my shrunken heart beginning to stretch; I felt levels of compassion I hadn't felt in years. And I thought of the sins that had previously tempted me with disbelief. *You mean I was allured by that? I must have been out of my mind!*

The sad thing about emotional depletion is that it makes sincere, godly people act as if they are "out of their minds." It twists personalities and alters behavior to the point where people become nearly unrecognizable to co-workers, friends, and spouses. Ultimately, it drives people to hurt those they love the most.

In contemporary Western culture we tend to view recreation as a luxury, as something to engage in if we have nothing important or productive to do. This isn't true for everyone, of course. Surely, some people reading these pages could justifiably accuse their spouses of being too devoted to recreation, or too "slowed down." Many people, however, would serve themselves, their spouses, and their families well by playing a few more games, by learning to relax, by discovering recreational outlets that refresh them. Far from being a luxury, it may be a necessary antidote to chronic emotional fatigue.

LET'S GET TOGETHER AGAIN

Another way to fill emotional tanks is by enjoying replenishing relationships.

Like us, you have probably been involved in three types of relationships. First, there are draining relationships, the kind that sap your energy. The people may be nice, but for some reason you don't click; or they always seem to want something from you and never offer anything back. During an hour spent with such a couple you check your watch six times, and after they leave you suggest to your spouse that you schedule your next get-together in the year 2025. It's not that you dislike them, but you always feel empty when they leave.

Next, there are neutral relationships. They don't drain you exactly; the people take a little, but they also give a little back in return, so it ends up being a wash. Still, such relationships don't really enhance your life and you're not highly motivated to maintain them.

Finally, there are replenishing relationships, which breathe life into you. You visit another couple, and after what seems like minutes you say, "I can't believe it's 11:30. Where did the evening go?" On the way home you wonder aloud to your spouse what your friends are doing next Friday night. You have no hidden agenda. You don't need anything from them, nor do you feel an obligatory responsibility toward them; you don't have to counsel or "fix" them. You just like being with them. You can prop your feet up on the coffee table and relax. You can talk freely. There's a natural ebb and flow in your relationship, and when you part ways everyone feels refreshed, energized, and lighthearted.

We have found that many people, particularly those in the helping professions, have some neutral relationships, many draining ones, and few, if any, replenishing friendships. Is it any wonder they feel emotionally depleted? Jesus seemed to be far more balanced in His relational world. He intentionally exposed himself to draining people—the masses who tugged at Him, sought healing, and asked an endless stream of questions. And He appeared to have some fairly neutral relationships with friends and disciples who followed Him but remained on the fringes of His life. But there also seemed to be a number of replenishing people in Jesus' life. He often slipped away with Peter, James, and John and frequently stopped by the home of Mary, Martha, and Lazarus. He needed time with people who replenished His spirit, and built Him up, and gave Him the freedom to relax. We think one reason Jesus broke down at Lazarus' tomb was that He had lost a replenishing brother.

Part of being a Christian is to give to those who can give nothing in return. If we claim to follow Jesus, we should intentionally pursue some draining relationships, as He did, and some neutral ones as well. But we must not overload our relational world with draining and neutral people. If Jesus needed replenishing relationships, how much more do we?

IT'S WORTH IT!

B Ending up in a teary pile on my desk on a busy Saturday afternoon was one of the best things that ever happened to me. Desperation made me face up to what crisis mode living and emotional depletion had done to me and to my relationships with the people I love, and it motivated me to do something about it.

It forced me to take one of the greatest ministry risks I have ever taken. It gave me the freedom to incorporate recreation into my life without feeling guilty about doing something so "unproductive." And it motivated me to get my relational life in better balance. It was obvious why I had little to offer Lynne and the kids: I was giving so much of my relational energy to draining people. I have since focused more attention on replenishing relationships, and they have recharged me and enhanced my marriage and family life.

It wasn't easy to make these changes, and there may be people who don't agree with the steps I've taken. But I can wholeheartedly say that getting out of crisis mode living was worth the price I had to pay. It is great to be relating to staff members as people again. To have friends who hold me accountable again. To have time to be actively involved with my kids again. To have creative energy to pour into my marriage again.

I'd like to shout it from the mountaintops: *It is worth whatever radical change it takes to get out of crisis mode. It is worth it!*

DARE TO DOWNSHIFT

Can you relate to this Achilles' heel? Are your emotional batteries low? Has your heart shrunk? Has the love drained out of your relationships? Do you think you might be heading for a crash?

If you are living in crisis mode, Beware. It *will* catch up with you, and it *will* undermine your marriage and family life. So please, don't rush from one emotionally draining activity to the next. Don't live so fast that you never have time for replenishing recreation or relationships. Don't neglect your need to trickle charge.

Perhaps you, too, need to make some radical changes in your life. Maybe you need to revise your job description. Or cut down on travel commitments. Maybe you need to resign from that board or drop that extra class. Another answer may be to refuse to take on so many projects, or hire some extra help, or downscale your goals. You may even have to take a demotion or say no to a wonderful opportunity—or a whole fistful of opportunities. How good, after all, is an opportunity that throws you into crisis mode? How great is a lifestyle that never gives you time to enjoy life?

In her cutting-edge book, *Downshifting*, Amy Saltzman, an associate editor for *U.S. News & World Report*, describes the "gracious romantic porches" that adorn the homes on Newark Street in Washington, D.C. She calls them "tailor-made for reading Faulkner, chatting with the neighbors, watching the world go by."[1] Yet she admits that during all her walks down Newark Street she had never seen anyone actually sitting on those enviably perfect porches. Successful young professionals dashed up and down the steps, but none had time to stop. That, Saltzman claims, "said it all" about the unhealthy pace of too many people's lives.

Saltzman suggests creative, practical ways for emotionally drained fast-trackers to "downshift" into more enjoyable patterns of life. People, she says, must redefine success in their own terms, and live according to those new images.

> "The new pictures in [downshifters'] heads are more eloquent, thoughtful and, ultimately, more satisfying. The front porch may not be as grand or the house it is attached to as large. But in this new picture, they are sitting on that porch, chatting with the neighbors, writing a letter to a friend and rereading that favorite old classic."[2]

People living in crisis mode rarely sit on front porches and chat with neighbors. They rarely write letters to friends or reread favorite books. And, may we add, they rarely have warm, satisfying marriages.

But we, like the downshifters in Saltzman's book, are living proof that such patterns can change.

WHAT ABOUT YOU?

Of course, you may not be living in crisis mode. Maybe the threat of emotional depletion isn't your Achilles' heel. But, unless you are a remarkable exception to the rule, you do have a weak spot. You do have an area of vulnerability.

Perhaps you have an uncontrollable temper fed by unresolved issues from your past, or childhood memories that haunt you and make you withdraw from your spouse. Maybe you have low self-esteem that causes you to become unreasonably jealous or insecure. Perhaps you don't relate well to your parents and you take out your frustration on your spouse.

If this chapter does nothing else, we hope it will motivate you to discover your Achilles' heel, acknowledge the negative effect it has on you as an individual and as a marriage partner, and take steps to become healthy, whole, and strong.

B We're not suggesting it will be easy or that changes can be made quickly. It took a solid year for me to make my journey back to wholeness. But at the end of that year, I felt like a different person. I had energy for life again. I was a contributor to my family again. I was excited about my marriage again.

And none too soon. Little did I know what was taking shape in the heart and mind of my long-suffering wife.

Notes

[1]Amy Saltzman, *Downshifting* (New York: Harper Collins Publishers, 1991), 13.
[2]Ibid., 224.

Twelve

Getting Lost Along the Way

"I love you. I just can't seem to handle being married to you. After sixteen years of marriage, I don't know who I am anymore. My life seems to have gotten lost in yours."

It was Thanksgiving evening. With the fragrance of a well-stuffed turkey still filling the house, the words tumbled out. But the issues that prompted them had begun to surface the previous May. In the early morning hours of what had been a sleepless spring night, I had poured out my heart to my computer.

"I can't go on like this," I wrote. "I can't live this life anymore. I keep rushing, rushing, rushing, rushing. I keep going, moving, doing, covering all the bases, responding to all the demands, the wishes, the suggestions, the oughts. I wish I could sleep for a week. I wish I could run away. But there are too many responsibilities. Bill is counting on me. I need to come through, like I always do.

"But I am so tired. I feel so empty. It's like someone drained the life out of me.

"I feel like a robot . . . but not quite. I wish I were a robot. Then I could just program myself to do everything I am supposed to do. And not care. And not desire. And not feel. And not hurt. And not have a little core of individuality that yelps occasionally.

"Is this what life is supposed to be? Is this the best I can do?"

Throughout the summer months the frustration, the emptiness, intensified. I felt increasingly like a vacuous shell, like an image with no substance. I realized, as I looked deep inside, that there was "nobody home." There was no person inside. No *me*.

191

L   I looked back through the years to a time when I had "existed." I saw a rosy newborn cradled in her father's arms. I saw a toddler spilling sand into buckets on a white beach. I saw a first-grader in a ribboned Easter bonnet standing ladylike by her mother's side. I saw a ten-year-old riding a pony across the green pasture behind an old farmhouse. I saw a teenager cheering for the Mustangs at a high school football game. I saw love and acceptance and fun and enthusiasm and happiness. I saw a childhood rich in the riches worth having.

So why, as an adult, did I feel so empty? So exhausted? So poor? So much like a . . . like a victim?

That was it! That was the word I had been looking for for months. I felt like a victim. A victim of life. A victim of Bill's life. His life had overpowered mine, swallowed up mine, erased mine.

CAUGHT IN THE AIR POCKET

Many people feel like victims of other people's behaviors and choices. Family members of alcoholics feel like victims of their loved one's drinking. Wives who are battered feel like victims of their spouse's uncontrollable temper. Some people feel like victims of another person's financial irresponsibility, or drug abuse, or unhealthy sexual desires. People with addictions or other compulsive disorders often litter the trail of their lives with friends and family members who feel like victims, who feel like their lives have been destroyed by another person's problem.

L   I didn't go so far as to say that my life had been destroyed. But I certainly felt that it had been sucked dry by Bill's overdevotion to work and ministry. We called it his Achilles' heel, but giving it a clever name didn't make it any less frustrating to me. I was tired of having to live with it.

Bill's work demanded nearly all his time and energy for many years. That meant I had to handle virtually every home/family/parenting responsibility. Did something break? Was someone sick? Did the bills have to be paid? Did the kids need a ride? Did something need to be

L cleaned, or bought, or cooked, or washed, or mowed, or maintained? Then I had to do it—or find someone to help me.

Even at the five-year point in our marriage, when Bill made a serious commitment to being home, that didn't change. He became more involved relationally with the kids and me, for which I was grateful. In fact, in many ways he became a model father; the kids did—and still do—adore him, feel very loved by him, and know they are a top priority to him: But he still had no time to devote to the practical, time-consuming, daily tasks of maintaining a home and family life.

In addition, there were the church responsibilities that "drew me in" simply because I was the minister's wife. There were people to relate to and events to attend and notes to answer and calls to return and parties to host.

Then there was Bill's speaking/traveling ministry. Though he tried to keep his travel schedule to a minimum, the opportunities became increasingly difficult to turn down. Often I joined him, either because it was a couples' event and my presence was expected, or because I feared the detachment caused by frequent separations. The net result was that I traveled far more than I wanted to, and spent innumerable hours making child-care arrangements, writing instructions, and repacking suitcases that became tattered from overuse.

I seemed to be constantly moving, working, striving. It wasn't that what I was doing was so awful. Some women would have been delighted to live my life. But it wasn't right for me. I was an introvert living an extroverted life. A slow-paced person in a constant rush. A homebody hopping planes. I lived with a constant stomachache—nervous butterflies that refused to be still. And I seldom got a good night's sleep. I often went to bed dreading the next day, and awoke disappointed that it had arrived so soon.

The biggest problem was that I seldom had time to do the things I wanted to do. I knew I had gifts and abilities, and at times throughout the years I tried to develop and use them. But that added so much rush and chaos to life

L that it was hardly worth it. Bill's work and gifts and pursuits so consumed me that I didn't have time for a life of my own. I felt more like an appendage to his life than a person in my own right.

Bill wasn't insensitive to the situation. Frequently during recent years he had urged me to make changes, to state my needs, to live how I wanted to live. But I didn't know where to start. I didn't know how to break the pattern. Bill raced through life, and repeatedly I got caught in the air pocket that trailed him.

I seemed to have no option, so I tried to accept it. But on an early morning in May I realized I couldn't accept it, and by midsummer I had begun to view myself as a victim. In the fall I felt something churning deep inside—something ugly and unwanted, something I couldn't control. I was angry with an anger that had been building for years.

I thought I had dealt with my anger. I thought the pain addressed in carefully constructed peace talks was all the pain there was. I thought the poisonous ooze that had broken through the surface occasionally was the extent of my hostility. Now I realized there was something deeper, buried beneath years of disappointment and frustration.

But suddenly it was refusing to stay buried. Suddenly it was exploding. And sobbing. And pounding. And shouting.

It was Thanksgiving day, and I was not thankful. I was bitter and resentful. I was tired of having to worry about *Bill's* needs, *Bill's* desires, *Bill's* convenience, *Bill's* plans. I was tired of helping him live his life and having no time or energy to live my own.

GIVING TILL IT HURTS

Those words grieve us. They are written in the past tense, but just barely. The pain they reveal is still fresh. The wounds have not yet healed. In fact, the ending to the story is only now being written.

We began working on this chapter on a blustering, Midwest morning in March. The previous weeks had been a flurry of ministry demands, out-of-state trips, and writing deadlines. It had been the kind of jumbled schedule that magnifies our temperament differences, highlights our communication weaknesses, and stretches our conflict resolution skills to the breaking point. We wore painted smiles to social functions, fulfilled our work responsibilities joylessly, and both fought the trapped feeling described in the early pages of this book. Romance had temporarily become a thing of the past.

When we finally had time to talk, it wasn't fun. We started facing one another at the kitchen table. We moved our discussion to the couch in the family room. We ended up seated on the bedroom floor, slumped against opposite walls.

We talked about our marriage and about the past. We talked about Thanksgiving and about anger. We talked about crisis mode and victims. The conversation was painful, shooting off on emotionally charged tangents and racing through two decades of relational mine fields. But it was also constructive. Peering through the tears, we discovered answers. We began to make sense out of the journey we'd been on together.

B We began to see how Lynne had fallen headlong into an unhealthy caretaker role. She had gotten so involved trying to take care of me, trying to rescue and protect me from the perils of crisis mode living, that she had neglected to take care of herself. She had ignored, or submerged, her needs, desires, feelings, and preferences. Finally, the neglect had caught up with her. She felt empty inside, she felt used and unappreciated, and understandably, she felt resentful.

Caretaking is a normal and healthy part of life. Parents are caretakers for their young children. Adult children often become caretakers for their elderly parents. Doctors and nurses are caretakers for the sick. Caretaking is healthy when we take care of those who legitimately need someone to take care of them— an infant or a sick friend, for example—and when we sincerely want to offer our help.

When we violate those guidelines, however, caretaking becomes unhealthy. When we do something we don't really want to do, when we say yes when we mean no, when we do things for people who are capable of and should be doing them for themselves, when we do more than our fair share when our help is requested, and when we fail to ask for what we want, need, and desire, we are involved in unhealthy caretaking, or rescuing.¹

People rescue other people for a variety of reasons. Some people have low self-esteem and only feel worthy when they are helping others. They need to be needed. They believe the only way to earn love is to serve ceaselessly.

Some people have been taught that if they refuse to help someone else they are selfish. They think it is wrong to disappoint someone or hurt their feelings by saying no. They have believed the lie that it is self-centered to think about themselves, and impolite to mention personal wants and needs.²

Women sometimes believe that constant caretaking is their duty. Good wives and mothers, they think, should devote themselves to caretaking no matter how old their children are or how capable their husbands are, and no matter how little time they have to care for themselves.

Others rescue because they believe it is a charitable deed, even a godly one. "Love your neighbor as yourself," the Bible says. "Go the extra mile." "Put on a heart of compassion." So they do. But they forget to love themselves in the process. They end up crawling the extra mile on weary hands and knees. They think it is cruel and cold-blooded to let people work through legitimate feelings, or suffer consequences of irresponsible behavior. So they let compassion turn to unhealthy caretaking.³

Acts of kindness and service are desirable. Giving what we want to give to those we love and to those who truly need our help is a privilege and a pleasure. Such acts make our homes, churches, and communities warm, inviting, life-giving places. But we need to establish limits in giving. "Giving to and doing things for and with people are essential parts of healthy living and healthy relationships," says counselor and author Melody Beattie. "But learning when not to give, when not to give in, and when not to do things for and with people are also essential parts of healthy living and healthy relationships."⁴

She adds that excessive caretakers "have misinterpreted the suggestions to 'give until it hurts.' We continue giving long after it hurts, usually until we are doubled over in pain. It's good to give some away, but we don't have to give it all away. It's okay to keep some for ourselves."⁵

OUR LIVES CLASHED ...

L   It wasn't hard to understand how I had slipped into excessive caregiving. I am by temperament compassionate and empathetic, so it was easy for me to push the biblical teaching on giving and loving to the outer limit. Also, I recognized that when I helped Bill carry his load I was ultimately helping the church and facilitating Bill's expanding ministry around the world. I think I could have stood up to the marketplace. If Bill had been in business I think I would have said, "For the sake of money, or position, or your ego, I won't do this." But it was for the advancement of God's kingdom. How could I say no to that?

My nearly ideal upbringing also made it hard for me to say no. I enjoyed a charmed childhood and a remarkably warm and peaceful home environment. There was an easy temperament blend between my parents and me and, therefore, little conflict. My parents encouraged me and cheered me on without pushing me, so I never felt an undue pressure to win their approval. I was responsible and never went through a rebellious era, so they were free to give me few rules, a flexible curfew, and an unusual measure of freedom. Compared to most parent/adolescent relationships, ours was a dream.

The only problem was that I never developed a fighting spirit. I never learned to confront people or to stand up for myself. I never learned to set limits, to say, "This is me. This is as far as I go. You can't push me any further." My home life was so safe, so easy, so comfortable, such a natural fit that I never had to learn those skills.

Then I married Bill, and the strength and independence and self-assurance that had initially drawn me to him began to overpower me. I loved him, but I didn't know how to stand up against his strength. I didn't know how to break through his independence. My self-assurance shriveled in the shadow of his.

Our temperaments clashed and I didn't know how to hang on to mine. Our preferences clashed and I didn't know how to assert mine. Our needs clashed and I didn't know how to get mine met.

Our lives clashed and I lost.

THIS IS ME!

One reason some people lose such battles is that they have failed to establish what psychologists call *boundaries*.

Dr. Henry Cloud says, "Boundaries are a property line. They define who we are and who we are not. . . . Boundaries give us a sense of limits as to what is part of us and what is not part of us, what we will allow and what we won't allow."⁶

Boundaries help us determine where we end and others begin, and what is our responsibility and what is someone else's. They help us determine how we will relate to others and protect us from being overpowered by others. Boundaries enable us to build close, vulnerable relationships with family members and friends without losing that very critical sense of separateness that defines who we are as individuals. People who fail to establish strong and healthy boundaries often end up feeling the kind of anguish described in the early pages of this chapter.

The most obvious aspect of personhood that lies within our boundaries is physical: Our physical body clearly defines us and separates us from others. Other aspects of our personhood may be less obvious, but are no less critical to our definition of who we are. These are our attitudes, our feelings, our behaviors, our thoughts, our abilities, our wants, our choices, our limits, and our negative assertions.

People with strong boundaries take responsibility for these aspects of their personhood. They admit their feelings—whether they are sad or mad or glad or scared—and deal with them. They discover their abilities and take active steps to develop them. They acknowledge their wants, express them, and, if appropriate, satisfy them. They make choices for themselves so that they don't become controlled by other people's choices. They know their limits and live within them, so they don't get overextended. They confidently make negative assertions: No, that isn't me. No, I don't want to do that. No, I don't like that. They know who they are, and they aren't afraid to let other people know who they are.

People with weak boundaries aren't quite so sure who they are. They are not in touch with their separateness from others. They don't understand where their responsibility for others ends and their responsibility for themselves begins. They often end up being more affected by what others feel, think, want, or choose, than what they feel, think, want, or choose themselves.

A SETUP

Learning about boundaries helped us understand some of the difficult dynamics in our marriage.

B   Growing up in my family, I had to develop a strong sense of boundaries. My dad had a very powerful personality. He was dominant, secure, confident, and intimidating to many people. His approval meant the world to me, but I realized at a young age that I could not afford to let his disapproval shape my choices. In order to survive under his authority, I had to risk standing up to him.

Though I never heard a definition of psychological boundaries when I was growing up, I definitely developed them. When I was nineteen years old, I put them to the ultimate test.

Early on a spring morning, I walked into his corner office and said, "Dad, this is a great company and I know you would like me to help run it. But God is calling me in a different direction. I think He wants me to go into Christian work. I'm leaving the business."

I walked out of his office shaking under the weight of his obvious displeasure and disappointment. I prayed, "God, what do I do? The person I respect and love more than anyone else on this planet has just said no to what You want me to say yes to. What am I going to do?"

I thought about twelve-year-old Jesus, standing in the synagogue in Jerusalem, informing Mary and Joseph that He had to pursue His "[Heavenly] Father's business."

I thought about the adult Jesus, startling His followers with these words: "If anyone comes to me and does not hate [love me more than] his father and mother, his wife and children, his brothers and sisters—yes, even his own life—he cannot be my disciple" (Luke 14:26).

B There is a time, the Bible seemed to be telling me, when you have to make up your own mind about things. You have to make your own choices about what to believe and who to follow. Someday you will stand accountable before a holy God, and you won't be able to hide in the shadow of your parents. So, step up to the plate and assume responsibility for your life. You're a big person. Make your own choice.

Several days later I went back into my dad's office and said, "Dad, you can cut me out of everything, if you have to—even a relationship with you. But I have to do what God is calling me to do. I would love to have your approval, and if you can't give it to me, I'm going to walk around with a gaping hole in my heart. But I am going to do what God is calling me to do."

That boundary battle marked my life. Though my dad died before he could see much of the fruit of my ministry, he did eventually support my decision. But even if he hadn't, I would have stood firm in my choice. I had learned to make tough decisions, to hold onto my opinions, and to fight for what I believed was right.

I acquired that ability in my youth, practiced it in young adulthood, and carried it with me into my ministry and into my marriage.

As Lynne said, she walked into marriage without having learned to stand up for herself, to claim her rights, to draw her boundaries. I, on the other hand, walked into marriage with my boundaries very clearly staked out. Is it any wonder Lynne's life got swallowed up in mine?

CROSSED BOUNDARIES

Excessive caretakers, or people with weak boundaries, often look extremely responsible—and they are—for other people. But they don't take responsibility for themselves. They tend to worry more about how others feel than how they feel, solve other people's problems instead of their own, yield to other people's desires and deny their own, and live with the consequences of other people's choices and fail to choose for themselves. They frequently take what others think more seriously than what they think, and often facilitate the development of other people's skills and abilities and neglect the development of their own. In short, they assume the responsibility for other people's success, welfare, and happiness, and fail to assume that same responsibility for themselves.

As we said earlier, they often believe that such behavior is right and necessary, perhaps even their Christian duty. But regardless of their motivation, they end up in the same unhappy condition: frustrated, angry, and resentful.

Excessive caretaking appears to be a loving thing to do. But it isn't. It actually produces what Melody Beattie calls a "triangle of hate." People rescue others in unhealthy ways. Later they get mad at those they have rescued because they felt forced to do things they didn't want to do. Then they feel used and sorry for themselves. This pattern fosters self-hate, and generates negative feelings toward other people.[7]

B For years I accused Lynne of not being supportive of me. It wasn't that she failed to help me in practical ways; on the contrary, she was constantly offering me her tangible support. But there was something unpleasant in her attitude toward me. She claimed to love me, but I often felt her disapproval, her dislike. It seemed as if she were angry with me much of the time.

Now I realize she was. She tried hard not to be, because she truly believed she was pleasing God by serving me. But she went too far and gave up too much of herself—her needs, her desires, her wants, her preferences. She had allowed me to cross her boundaries, and the anger was inevitable. Even though she tried to pray it away, it lingered. Even though she tried to bury it, it leached through her layers of good intentions and tainted our relationship. Eventually, it exploded.

TAKING CARE OF *ME*

Many relationships are laced with the anger of crossed boundaries. Many people resent the fact that their parent or child or spouse always gets his or her way. They resent feeling that they have to rescue people. They resent never having the time or freedom to live their own life. But that can change. There is a way to move out of resentment.

It is called personal empowerment. It means that people start taking care of themselves. They reclaim the responsibility for their lives, for their happiness, and for their future. They own their plight. They quit focusing on what someone else has done to them and start thinking about what they need to do for themselves. They start behaving as adults and making choices they can live with. They give themselves permission to feel their feelings. They start doing what they want to do. They admit their needs, and when appropriate, ask other people to help meet their needs. They quit calling themselves victims—and quit acting like victims.

Many of these victims really were true victims at some point in their lives: victims of abuse, neglect, abandonment, alcoholism, or some other situation against which they truly were helpless to protect themselves. But many people perpetuate their victimization, or even create it, by *allowing* other people to take advantage of them. Part of their healing process is to acknowledge their part in their victimization.[8] If they helped get themselves into the situation they are in, it follows that they have the power to get themselves out.

Dr. Cloud says,

> "As an adult, you have choices. Take responsibility for them and own them. If you are giving something, you at some level are making a choice to do it; stop acting as if others make you give to them. If you are working somewhere that you do not like, take responsibility for finding something else. If you are criticized by a friend, take responsibility for the fact that you agree to meet with him or her. You are responsible for what you choose to do. *You can change your life by refusing to play victim* [italics ours]."[9]

Another part of the healing process is for victims to forgive those who have truly caused hurt or offense, or who have taken advantage of them. Most people who feel victimized have tried forgiveness—time and time again. But each time the anger and resentment return, they realize that their attempt to forgive didn't work. Obviously, they assume, they weren't sincere or caring or godly enough; so on top of their other troubles they heap loads of guilt. Often, however, the real reason their forgiveness doesn't "work" is that they are still allowing the other person to hurt them, or take advantage of them, or overpower them. Only when they begin taking responsibility for their lives, and crawl out from under the burden of another person's problem, can they really forgive. Melody Beattie says, "Forgiveness comes in time—in its own time—if we are striving to take care of ourselves. . . . If we are taking care of us, we will understand what to forgive and when it's time to do that."[10]

When we start acting like adults and taking responsibility for our lives, we force other people to act like adults too, and to face the consequences of their actions. This is better for us, and it ends up being better for them too.

L   I realize now that one reason Bill lived in crisis mode for so long was that I "enabled" him to. By pouring my time and energy into picking up the pieces of his whirlwind life, I made it possible for him to continue the unhealthy pace. He could devote ninety percent of his energy into work and still have an orderly, well-maintained refuge to come home to because I kept it that way. He could maintain great relationships with the kids because I kept close track of them and warned him when one of them had a special need or was beginning to feel neglected. He could schedule back-to-back trips because I scrambled to get him ready to go again and covered all the bases while he was gone. I didn't want to do all those things, but I did them anyway.

It would have been better for me and for him if I had quit caretaking years ago—or better yet, had never started. I wouldn't have gotten lost along the way, and perhaps Bill wouldn't have pushed himself until he crashed.

YOU CAN'T LOVE WHAT ISN'T THERE

Some people get lost along the way because they have low self-esteem. Others end up with low self-esteem because they got lost along the way. For years they treat others as if they are more important than themselves, and eventually they begin to believe it.

L   I have long been aware of my sagging self-esteem. But I couldn't understand where it came from. I grew up in a loving, warm, supportive family. My parents are still the two biggest cheerleaders in my life. They always told me I could do anything or be anything or accomplish anything I wished. As a teenager and young adult I was positive and cheerful and happy.

So why, I often wondered, *do I feel like such a failure now? Why do I dislike myself so much?*

I realize now that throughout my adult years I gave so much of myself away that eventually there was little left for me to feel good about. There was little left to love.

It wasn't just because I was taking too much responsibility for Bill's life. I was busy trying to please everyone else, too. That often happens to Christian leaders. They know people are looking at them and they don't want to offend anybody, so they play it safe. They watch how they dress and what they drive. They watch what they say and to whom they say it. They watch how they spend their time and where they spend their money. They do their best to respond to everyone's requests and satisfy everyone's demands. Pretty soon, they become little more than a reflection of others' expectations. They don't know what they want anymore—or who they are. They have lost their individuality, and they don't like what is left.

YOU CAN'T HUG AIR

Nobody wins when someone gets lost along the way.

The "lost" person loses. He or she ends up feeling like a victim and enduring an unhappy existence.

God loses, even if the person got lost "for His sake," because we can only really give ourselves to God if we have a self to give. We can only serve Him wholeheartedly if we serve Him joyfully. We can only love Him sincerely if we love Him out of peace-filled, grateful hearts. If we are unhappy with our lives we will probably be unhappy with God. If we feel like victims, we will probably, on some level, blame Him.

And spouses lose too, even if they were beneficiaries of heroic caretaking or if they were rescued time and time again. They lose because they end up married to an empty person. They end up loving a mirage. And it's hard to love a mirage. You can't hug air.

Loving doesn't mean we submerge our personhood in someone else's. Making a marriage work doesn't mean we have to give up who we are. The goal of a healthy marriage is for both spouses to maintain their individuality and bring their unique and valuable contributions to the relationship. We fell short of that goal and we both paid. But no more.

L   I have been very open with Todd and Shauna about the journey I have been on recently. When they want to encourage me along the path they say, "Get a life, Mom. Get a life!"

That's what I'm doing.

I have dramatically reduced the pace of my life by learning to say no. I am asking Bill for more help on the home front and receiving an enthusiastic, willing response. I am traveling less and liking it more. I have crawled out from under unreasonable relational expectations and narrowed my circle of close friends. I am "treating myself," to nature—walking forest preserve trails, driving down country roads, photographing wildflowers—just because I enjoy it. I am spending more time with my extended family. I am making time to write.

And I am loving it! I am experiencing a level of happiness that I haven't known in years. My stomachache disappeared and I am sleeping better. I feel productive and fulfilled. I am having a great time with my kids. My relationship with God is more authentic than it has ever been.

And my marriage? Let me just say that the only person happier about these changes than I am is Bill.

REAPING THE REWARDS

Crisis mode living and unhealthy caretaking took a toll on our marriage for years. We worked hard in many areas and made a lot of progress. But all the while a subterranean stream of tension and hurt meandered deep down in the loamy soil of our relationship. We look back and think, *If only we had known. If only we had understood what we were doing. If only we had made changes sooner.*

But we also look forward. And when we do, we nearly burst with hope. We feel as if we are entering a new era. We've paid the price of self-discovery; now we get to reap the rewards. We know we will still sin, and sometimes hurt one another, and vacillate between extremes. But in a very dramatic way, we are different people now than we were before. We are both living more consistently with how God made us. We have acknowledged our Achilles' heels and our unhealthy behaviors, and we have made changes. We are happier, healthier individuals, and that frees us to be more loving spouses.

This morning we sat in a sunlit coffee shop and thanked one another for growing, for working, and for enduring. We both know a lot about enduring. Enduring means refusing to give up in the middle of a crisis, and being humble enough to ask for help. It means trudging along when you don't see the light at the end of the tunnel, and holding on when you don't want to. In the few remaining pages of this book we want to highlight a few specific principles that helped us endure during difficult days.

Notes

[1]Melody Beattie, *Codependent No More* (San Francisco: Harper & Row Publishers, 1987), 78.

[2]Ibid., 79.

[3]Ibid., 84.

[4]Ibid., 87.

[5]Ibid., 86.

[6]Dr. Henry Cloud, *When Your World Makes No Sense* (Nashville: Thomas Nelson Publishers, 1990), 105.

[7]Beattie, *Codependent No More*, 81.
[8]Ibid., 80.
[9]Cloud, *When Your World Makes No Sense*, 177.
[10]Beattie, *Codependent No More*, 198.

Thirteen

Staying Together When Life Is Tearing You Apart

Few marriages as difficult as ours survive. In fact, the closer we look at our marriage, the more amazed we are that it has survived. Love and respect had drawn us to one another, and on May 18, 1974, we joined hands and vowed to walk through life together. But before we celebrated our first anniversary, our different family backgrounds and temperaments had begun to pull us apart. Poor conflict resolution skills further strained our clutching hands. We held on for dear life, but when the romance in our marriage began to die, we nearly lost our grip. Crisis mode living and unhealthy caretaking made it even harder to hold on. We choked on the bile of hidden hostilities and didn't want to hold on. We reached painful impasses, and wondered if it was worth holding on.

But we held on. We stayed together when life was tearing us apart, and we ended up with a solid, healthy marriage that is getting better every day.

But why have we managed to hold on when so many people haven't? Was it raw strength? Willpower? Did we know how to grit our teeth better than the rest? Or were there other factors that gave us an edge and kept us from giving up too soon? During a recent Thursday morning breakfast date, we asked each other those questions. We want to end this book with our answers.

A LIFE-CHANGING DIFFERENCE

The first answer we both gave takes us back nearly to the beginning of this book. We hate to be repetitious, but we can't deny the truth. What helped us hold on more than anything else was that we maintained spiritual authenticity. We looked for truth and guidance in the Bible. We memorized verses that encouraged us to be kind, loving, honest, and patient. We prayed for help. We begged God to give us insight and understanding and creative ideas. We asked ourselves again and again, "What does God want us to do now? How would Jesus handle this situation? What attitude would He have? What words would He say?" We tried our best to obey God, and when we failed to, we repented. Many times we didn't want to do those things. Sometimes, in fact, we both wished we weren't Christians. We wished that pleasing God didn't matter to us. We wished we could be hard-hearted without feeling bad about it. We wished we could slam doors without regretting it. And turn our backs on our spouses without hearing a divine whisper: *Don't do that. You'll be sorry. You have too much to lose.* Sometimes we would have given anything not to have to do the right thing.

But submitting ourselves to God, even as halfheartedly and unhappily as we sometimes did, kept our hearts soft. It didn't make us perfect—far from it—but it made us flexible and humble. It kept us on the right track. It kept us working at marriage.

If your Christianity is merely a matter of talk, we challenge you to take it further. Let it change your life. Study the Bible. Pray. Obey God. See what a difference it can make in your marriage.

If you aren't a Christian, please examine the truths of Christianity with an open mind. Jesus Christ died to free all of us from the tyranny of sin and to reconcile us to God and to one another.

If you are a Christian, but your spouse isn't, please make your continued spiritual growth a priority. You cannot change your spouse, but you can change yourself. You can tap God's power to a greater degree, and become stronger and more loving and more mature. Then you can pray earnestly that your spouse will one day choose to submit to the God you have submitted to.

WHAT CAN WE LEARN?

We also agreed that taking advantage of the wonderful self-help resources available today greatly increased our holding power. We went to seminars and workshops and conferences on marriage. We listened to tapes on marriage. We read books on marriage.

Oh, did we read books! We read together and read separately. We read on vacation and read ourselves to sleep at night. We read books by theologians and psychologists and marriage counselors. We read about temperaments, personal growth, workaholism, conflict resolution, sex, stress management, how to relax, how to raise kids, how to handle money. We latched on to every good idea we could find, and it helped tremendously.

Some people give up before they read the first book, or listen to the first tape, or attend the first workshop. That's a tragedy. Only we are to blame if we fail to use the incredible resources at our disposal.

We also benefited from being in a church that put strong emphasis on marriage and family life. If your church doesn't provide challenging, insightful, practical teaching that helps you become a better spouse, perhaps another church could serve you better.

HOLD US ACCOUNTABLE

One of the wisest choices we made was to open our marriage to the scrutiny of close friends. We have always had someone, usually a couple, with whom we could discuss the truth about our relationship, with whom we could say, "We had a terrible fight last night and we're hurting." Or, "We are stuck and we need help." Or, "We are discouraged. We've been working so hard and getting nowhere."

Sometimes we just needed a safe place to blow off steam so we could settle down and talk constructively. At other times we needed advice from people who knew and loved both of us. We often needed somebody to cheer us on, to root for us, to say, "We love you two, and we know you can make it through this. You have so much invested in this marriage. Keep trying. It'll be worth it."

Coming to grips with crisis mode living and unhealthy caretaking were the greatest breakthroughs of our adult lives. We are very thankful for the loving couple who went on the sometimes painful, sometimes exhilarating journey with us. Many times we needed the perspective of outside observers. Often they helped us sort through our jumble of tangled insights and put our thoughts into words. They rejoiced when we made progress, and grieved when we didn't. They took care of our kids when we needed time alone. They sat through silly movies when we needed to laugh. They held us accountable when they saw us slipping.

"How's your schedule, Bill? Are you keeping it under control?"

"Are you taking care of yourself, Lynne? Are you being honest about what you need?"

Most people in past generations were hesitant to be vulnerable, particularly in regard to marriage. "We're doing just fine," they'd say. "Just fine." We chose the opposite approach: to be open, to invite a few trustworthy, proven friends inside our relationship. We think it was a wise choice and encourage you to do the same.

If you and your spouse are not close to another couple, we challenge you to begin now to build such a friendship. You could join a couples' group at your church or invite some couples over for dinner. When you discover a husband and wife you both enjoy spending time with, meet with them again. If the four of you continue to "click," you have a foundation to build on. If you don't, you can try someone else. You won't build a solid couples' friendship overnight; it will take an investment of time and effort. But it may be one of the best things you ever do for your marriage.

REMEMBER WHEN . . .

Identifying a few activities that minimized our differences and provided a respite from our struggles also helped us hold on. We discovered, for example, that we enjoy driving long distances together. As different as we are, when we cloister ourselves within the confines of a car, we seem to mesh easily. Maybe it's because we are forced to travel at the same pace. Maybe it's because we are isolated from outside pressures. Whatever the reason, we both become unusually easygoing and lighthearted, our conversations ambling pleasantly off on interesting side roads and unexpected detours. We both enjoy winding our way through rural towns and eating lunch in down-home diners. We always feel that we're a mile or two ahead of responsibility and just out of reach of real life.

Sailing does the same for us, to an even greater degree. We don't own a boat, but gracious friends often let us use theirs. We always have a wonderful time. We trim the sails, set our course, and feel like we are in paradise. Shortly after one particularly enjoyable trip, we entered one of the roughest eras of our marriage. We both felt like giving up, but we kept remembering how well we had gotten along on the sailing trip. We kept remembering the laughter and the romance, and that memory propelled us into the future. Reminding ourselves of the happiness we had known then motivated us to recapture it.

Vacations, getaways, recreation, and fun sometimes make the difference between letting go and hanging on. Creating pleasant memories doesn't have to cost a lot of money, but the result can be priceless.

PAINFUL REALITIES

Ministers and their spouses hear more than a normal share of sad stories. People pour out their hearts in phone calls and letters and counseling sessions. As grieved as we have been by these accumulated tragedies, hearing them has helped us by giving us a glimpse of reality.

Some people imagine divorce as an easy way out, but we learned through other people's experiences that husbands, wives, and children all pay a heavy price when marriages fail. People who opt for divorce unwittingly trade one set of problems for another, and the postdivorce problems are often far harder to resolve than the marital problems would have been. A divorce lawyer told us that most couples he deals with say they wish they had worked to build their marriages as hard as they have to work to survive divorce.

Working through a difficult marriage may be painful, but usually not as painful as giving up. Each time we got weary of the work, we thought of the stories we had heard and the devastation we had seen, and we found strength to hold on a little longer.

HOW TO CRY FOR HELP

Problems, conflicts, and differences can lead to divorce court, but they don't have to if couples learn how to seek constructive help.

A woman we know who committed adultery said, "I was miserable, and I didn't think I had any options. I didn't know how to cry for help. Finally, I couldn't stand it anymore . . . so I did something stupid." Because she was a leader in her church, she was afraid to admit to her friends how troubled her marriage was. She was also afraid of the stigma of going to a counselor. So she did nothing, until she couldn't hold on any longer, and she sought help in another man's bed.

Instead of getting so desperate that we committed adultery, or ran away, or did some other destructive thing, we found legitimate ways to cry for help. We poured out our frustrations to God and sought His help. We were honest with each other about how desperate we sometimes felt, even saying difficult things like, "I'm drifting away from you. I'm being tempted by other people. We need to do something about this." We picked up the books again. We talked to friends. Again, watching other people travel the downward spiral all the way to the bottom made us determined to do *whatever we had to do* to avoid descending into desperation.

For many couples, professional counseling may be the best way to cry for help. It grieves us that so many people in faltering marriages hesitate to seek counsel. We firmly believe that many estranged couples could have avoided appointments with the divorce lawyer had they scheduled appointments with a marriage counselor soon enough.

A temporary separation may be helpful for other couples. We suggest separation not as an alternative to marriage, but as an alternative to divorce. We have known husbands and wives who were so frustrated and hurt by marital conflicts that they truly wanted out of their marriages. However, after a period of separation under the guidance of a wise counselor, they were able to reconcile with their spouse and rebuild their relationship. A time of individual healing often enables spouses to face the challenge of marriage later, with renewed energy and wisdom.

A separation is probably necessary if there is any form of physical abuse taking place in a marriage, and often advisable when there is substance abuse involved. Scripture repeatedly affirms the sanctity and permanence of marriage, and this book is dedicated to helping married people stay together. But the Bible also eloquently proclaims the worth of the individual, denounces violence, and calls for Christians to respond with compassion and kindness to those who have been oppressed or harmed or taken advantage of. It is in that spirit of Christian compassion that we encourage spouses in abusive situations to temporarily get out and to cry for help as loudly as they can.

CALL IT COMMITMENT

For us, the final key to holding on was learning not to panic every time we hit a crisis.

When we are getting along well we say we are *connecting*. When we are connected we love being together, we talk easily and laugh freely, we touch each other naturally and lovingly, we encourage each other, we celebrate each other's uniqueness, we serve each other joyfully, and we tease each other playfully. Connection is the goal of marriage; it is the oneness the Bible talks about. It's wonderful, it's happy, and it's fun.

But we discovered long ago that it takes precious little for us to *disconnect*. Sin, temperament differences, exhaustion, outside pressures, the demands of life—any one or all of these can push us into a way of relating that is anything but wonderful and happy and fun.

Early in our marriage, whenever we disconnected, we panicked. We thought any slip from perfect oneness signaled disaster. We were on the ropes. Divorce was inevitable. We might as well tag the furniture and divvy up the silverware. There was no hope and no turning back. We felt like we were caught in an angry current, destined for a deadly crash on a rocky reef. We always managed to avoid the crash—just in the nick of time—but that didn't lessen our fear of disconnection.

Then one night, during a sensitive discussion of our then-current disconnection, we realized that because we both meant our wedding vows, had a spirit of reconciliation, and were willing to plow through the work of conflict resolution, we did not have to panic over disconnection. We did not have to assume we were headed for ruin. We could untag the furniture and put away the silver. We weren't going anywhere. We were *committed* to one another.

That made a tremendous difference to us. We quit thinking of disconnection as a precursor of disaster, and quit predicting gloom and doom. We began to call disconnection the "commitment phase." Instead of focusing on the negative, we reminded one another of the positive: In spite of the difficulty we were facing, we had a rock-solid commitment to one another that would see us through disconnection and back into oneness.

Being imperfect people in an imperfect marriage, we are going to disconnect periodically. And living in a busy world means that we can't always rush right out for a three-hour dinner to figure out what went wrong. Sometimes it may be two or three days before we can fully address the real issues. That is when the commitment phase serves us well. During those awkward hours of waiting we keep reminding ourselves of our mutual commitment. Yes, there is a problem. Yes, it might be serious. But we don't have to slide to the edge of ruin because of it. We're not going to do anything destructive or stupid. We are going to pray fervently for one another, we are going to treat each other respectfully and courteously, and we are going to work our way back to connection.

The commitment phase is not the goal of marriage or what courting couples dream about. It doesn't hold a candle to romance. But it is a far better alternative than despair. It is, in essence, an affirmation of hope. It is a noble, valiant refusal to give up. It is a wide-angle view of life, a disciplined willingness to fix our sights beyond the problem at hand and focus on the reality of future reconnection.

When we were twenty-two, love and unbridled optimism convinced us that we were more than ready to become ideal spouses. We were, or so we believed, fit to be tied.* By thirty-two, we had been initiated into reality many times over. Fights and frustrations had led to anguish and anger. We had had it. We

---

* *'Fit to be tied' is also a colloquial expression, often used in America, meaning 'angry enough to burst'.*

were fit to be tied.

Now we stand on the edge of another decade. We are less idealistic than we were at twenty-two, but far happier than we were at thirty-two. We have fought battles and jumped hurdles and learned lessons and held on. And now we can say confidently what we said naively years ago: We really *are* fit to be tied.